VICTORY'S ROAD

A Graceful Drive Through Life's Obstacles

Nicole C. Calhoun

RTS
PenPoint
Publications
A Division of Restored to Stand Ministries

Nicole C. Calhoun/RTS PenPoint Publications
nicole@restoredtostand.com
www.nicolecalhoun.com

Book Layout ©2013 BookDesignTemplates.com

Ordering Information:
Quantity sales. Special discounts are available on quantity purchases
by corporations, associations, and others. For details, contact the
"Special Sales Department" at the address above.

Victory's Road/ Nicole C. Calhoun. —3rd ed.
ISBN 978-0-9905423-3-9

This book is dedicated to my mom, Nadine Talley. You have always believed in and supported me. Thank you for sacrificing yourself to raise four children on your own. You demonstrated to me the importance of moving forward even when it is not easy. You never gave up, but always kept going in spite of every challenge. I love you.

CONTENTS

ACKNOWLEDGEMENTS

With special thanks to my husband, Sekou "Kenneth" Calhoun and sons who were patient as I spent hours making updates to this version of the book. I love and appreciate you guys so much!

PREFACE

If you picked up this book, my guess is you have encountered your fair share of challenges thus far. And you want to see a clear path ahead. Am I right? If so, I want to tell you a short story of how this book came to be. This story will give you a glimmer of hope of the victory ahead of you through Christ.

I was twenty-eight-years-old when I finally admitted that I needed a Savior. I remember it like it was yesterday. It was on a bright summer day. I got up that morning, determined to visit a friend's church. Until then, I rarely attended church services because I felt I was not ready to commit. The truth is I thought I was too much of a sinner. I knew my life did not reflect what God wanted for me. I had always said that I wanted to "get myself together" first. This day was different, however, and I wanted change. I had been carrying around the baggage of a broken heart for more than a few years. I was tired, and made up in my mind that day that I was going. I had no expectations nor a clue that my life was about to drastically alter.

I put on a navy blue, knee-length sundress with a white summer sweater. I remember the morning was warm because I had sprinkled on so much powder that someone at the church noticed and discreetly advised me that it was showing. I still laugh when I think about it. The church had beautiful column windows along each side of the sanctuary that let the sunlight in. Though the church held about 500 occupants, I felt right at home. It was as if God made that day perfectly just for me. The smile I wore reflected the day's beauty more so than how I felt inside. Actually, I had mastered how to look on the outside. Internally, I was in turmoil. I felt alone, unwanted, and unloved. I hit an all-time low, and was ready for something or Someone who could lift me up.

Amazingly, it was as if the minister spoke directly to me. I thought, *How could he know my situation? Who could have told him?* I knew God had set me up to be in the right place at the right time. It was His way of giving me what I was missing: hope. I never felt God's love so tangibly before this moment. That day, I decided it was time to give it all to Jesus Christ. I gave Him all of the baggage, all of the pain, and all of my heart. It was by far the best thing that ever happened to me.

This change became an adventure. I wanted to know *why* I believed in Jesus Christ. There was so much to learn, so much to discover. I went on a quest to consume the entire Bible every chance I got. I would stay up late, reading, because I could not put it down. I was hungry for truth. I soon found that because of my hunger, God taught me many life lessons that dealt with the turmoil I had been carrying. Through them, He gracefully began peeling back so many layers that needed removal. He did this in a way that only a loving Father can, reassuringly and delicately. I know these lessons are the catalyst that took me from a broken-hearted, bitter, angry woman, to one who now had newfound hope in Someone greater than herself.

These lessons have been so valuable for me that I wanted to share them with you. I want to share them with anyone who needs the hope that God can navigate their life through the obstacles. I want to shout from the roof tops that He will take your life and put you on a track that only ends victoriously. Now that you are here and ready, let's begin down this journey to victory.

INTRODUCTION

It was one of those of bitterly cold days. Snow had blanketed everything in sight, a typical winter in Detroit. My mom, hurried to get out the door. She had to drop me at daycare and make it to work on time. Despite the bad weather, she could not afford to be late; she carried the sole responsibility of caring for me. She hurriedly cleared just enough frost from the car window to see while driving. She hopped in the car. I was already seated in the passenger seat and eating my breakfast. She started the car, took off, and CRASH! She hit a parked car, and I remember saying, "You made me drop my food." You have to forgive me, I was about four- or five-years-old and didn't know any better. Needless to say, it was my first accident, at least the first I can remember. I do not remember much about how she got to work or if she made it at all. However, as I reflect on the experience, it was one of my first-known obstacles and setbacks in life. That day, my mom tried her best to fulfill her obligations, yet she could not because that unforeseen accident occurred. I have discovered that's pretty much the way of life.

While I have used a very common occurrence to demonstrate how life can consist of many surprises, my personal experiences extend well beyond a fender bender. You will find throughout this book my testimonies of how God navigated me through my life—past and present—to bring me to His truth. Testimonies of growing up without a father, of living in battered women shelters, and witnessing those I love slowly kill themselves through alcohol and drug abuse. I will also share stories of my poor decisions and their consequences. I will share some treasures of grace and mercy through others that God placed before me while on this journey. At just the right time, I finally came to the end of myself and was tired of handling life on my own. I was ready to let God take control.

You are likely reading this book because you have come to a place in your life where you have grown tired of being driven off your path by circumstances. You may be feeling like no matter how much you try to avoid life's mishaps, they happen to you. In fact, it feels like they are hunting you down! I want to pose a question: Are you willing to come to the realization that trials and tribulations are a part of life? I would encourage you that accepting this fact will help you greatly. Hear me out before you become frustrated because this acceptance will ultimately encourage you. Why? Because in all honesty, we cannot control what occurs around us. Believe me. I have tried to some degree. Instead, you and I must learn how to maneuver around the obstacles when they appear. How do you keep going with grace and finesse instead of falling apart as before? The answer is in allowing God to be the Director of your journey.

It was not until I came to Christ that I learned I did not have to take this journey alone; nor did I have to go in my own strength. In fact, I learned these roads I have travelled could lead to a victory that I never could have imagined. I have learned this journey could result in growth and development in Christ if I allow it. While I am in no way at the end of this journey to victory, I am now able to see the obstacles as tools and opportunities to shape me.

This book is intended to aid you in your journey. It will give you hope of the victory ahead of you. Let this book be your daily devotion for a period of time. Proactively apply the lessons of this book. Take your time to ponder on them. Let God set the pace. Remember, our faith comes from hearing God's Word. Get the most out of this book by leveraging the value of the scriptures included within each chapter. Allow yourself to discover that His Word has the power to change your life and your situations. Make sure you keep a journal close by to record your own thoughts and lessons. Be encouraged that you are not alone on this journey. Christ is with you.

Now, let's travel Victory's Road.

TRUE LIFE IS FOUND IN CHRIST

Hearing by the Word of God...

"In Him is Life and That Life is the Light of Men"
(John 1:4).

"Mommy, what did your mom look like"? That was the question I asked my mother as a child. My maternal grandmother had long passed when my mom was eight-years-old. There were no surviving pictures of her, so occasionally I would wonder about her. She must have been beautiful because my Mom was beautiful. Did she look like my mom? Did I look like her? I had so many questions. Barely in her thirties, my maternal grandmother left behind four young children to grow up in the foster system. There were two boys and two girls, "stair steps," they used to say, because they were each one year apart from the next. Each of the siblings took their turns being passed around several foster homes. From the stories my mom told, this way of life was not ideal, at least not in the sixties. Ultimately, feeling she had no other choice, she left her final foster family at the age of seventeen. This is where my life began.

What is Life?

Do we really know what it is or what to do with it? We know we are alive and here. But why? Is there a goal to keep in mind? Is our sole purpose to live many years and then die? Is it to focus on our desires or that of others? Most of us do not know these answers, so we resort to survival mode.

If we were to be honest, we would admit that much of our lives have been aimless and without purpose. That is, we are here and surviving. We have a sense of goals, but our goals and aspirations are usually purely for self-gain. You and I both know it is easy to live for selfish ambition. Who could blame us? The media does a good job of letting us know who we should be and what we should have. Societal norms have made life about making money, buying material goods, and finding happiness. We search for fulfillment in things that are temporary, things that will be left behind once we have passed on.

Regrettably, our hunger for contentment can never be fully satisfied by material gain, so goes the downward spiral. Thousands of years after the book of Ecclesiastes was written, we are still "chasing after the wind." Unfortunately, with this endless pursuit of temporal satisfaction comes much sorrow and regret. Little do we realize, we are chasing after the wrong things. We do not want temporary gratification. However, what the world has to offer is only temporary. We want eternal satisfaction. This type of satisfaction can only be found in true life. "What is true life?" you ask. True life is found in Christ. With all of this in mind, we should really try to find the Possessor of true life (John 1:4).

Chasing after the Wind

I am guilty of living most of my twenties chasing after gratification. Ironically, instead of being grateful, I suffered the opposite. In the preface of this book, I mentioned how I came to Christ broken-hearted. You might wonder how I got there. How did my heart get so broken that I felt it was shattered into tiny pieces? I think a therapist would say the absence of my father was the primary factor; and I'm sure that played somewhat of a role. My guess is the vast majority of heartbreak was caused by jumping in and out of relationships. Yep, that pretty much did it! Like many, my life has been full of mistakes. My personal struggle was in longing for the companionship of a husband; and maybe it was because I had no father figure. Admittedly, I lost my virginity in my early teens, much too young for a girl to understand sex. I was not what people would call a "fast girl." I simply wanted to be loved and accepted. The older I got, I began meeting di erent men. I hoped for each one to be a part of the love that my heart so yearned. Each time proved to be a failure. Continuing down this path, I made bad decisions, giving myself to them intimately. I did things out of character, outrageous things. And I justified them in the name of fun and fulfillment. I had no real purpose. I "[chased] after the wind."

Hitting Rock Bottom

Certainly, after years of this self-deception, it took an emotional toll on me. I found myself bitter and depressed. I blamed everyone else for the pain that I felt. And at the time, it never occurred to me that this pain was a result of the "fun and fulfilling life" I had chosen. From the outside, I appeared to have the "total package;" but inside I was so lost and falling apart. I accomplished what society deemed as success: a degree, a good-paying job, a house, a car. But the emptiness would not leave. It only increased with each failed relationship.

I started feeling used and thrown out like dirty laundry. Bitterness and negativity had taken over my thinking. "How on earth can these guys keep getting away with what they are doing?" I asked myself. They seemed to go from one person to the next, leaving a trail of broken hearts and wounded souls. Inevitably, I found myself mad at God, as if to say that He had something to do with my bad decisions.

I began lowering my standards, as if they were not low enough. I began compromising and telling myself that I did not need to get married; that I could just date without feelings; but I found that I was only fooling myself. I finally came to my lowest point. I was bitter and depressed.

Fed up with the heaviness, I talked to a friend over the phone about my situation. I cried and cried the entire time; and as I spoke with her, she said something totally unexpected: "I see you do not have a relationship with God." I remember thinking, *She does not know what she is talking about. I pray.* Then what she said made me think; it also made me realize just how low I had sunk; and from that moment, my eyes were opened.

My problems were not rooted within the actions of others but within myself.

I Found Life

Finally having rededicated my life to God, He began showing me so many wonderful things, which began my new journey. I made the decision to give up my old life, and this was probably one of the easiest decisions I ever made. I was so broken; I did not want that life anymore; I wanted God. Determined to learn about Him, I went on a quest to read the entire Bible, which opened the door to my lessons.

I learned that the emotional toll I experienced was caused by my personal decisions, which ignored God's Word; and God's Word is life (see John 17:17). I committed the very things that He commanded me not to do; and I rationalized that God did not want me to have fun. I learned that life in Him was not boring; in fact, the Christian life is exhilarating. I learned that He wants us to recognize the consequences of a sinful lifestyle.

The Bible is not meant to keep you from enjoying the fun parts of life; but it is a book of instructions that prevent us from distracting ourselves from our true purpose. Think about some of the problems in the world like sexually transmitted diseases, teenage pregnancy, crime, hunger, homelessness, and other modern struggles. Did you know the Bible addresses every one of these things? For example, the Bible tells us not to have premarital sex, and we think, *Well, why not?* It is not too hard to determine these reasons, and more of them reveal themselves every day, even to nonbelievers. Think of the troublesome effects of STDs, unwanted pregnancies, abortions, and abandoned children. These things are not life, not the true life that Christ brings. They are certainly not what God wants us to go through. God is not trying to suppress our enjoyment. He is trying to lead us to a path that is free from the consequences that come as a result of sinful acts. Do not misunderstand: not all fun involves sin. Not all sin is really fun; it just appears to be that way. God is really protecting us, and why is this? It is because He loves us.

What about You?

So many have similar stories of hurt, longing, betrayal, or cruelty. Maybe even you. Whatever the case may be, the emotional damage from these occurrences still negatively a ects us. I have found that most people are hurting as a result of bad choices. However, the hurt does not have to remain. On a number of occasions, God has worked what I would consider miracles within me. Finding life in Christ has by far been the most memorable and most drastic. People have asked me, "What did you do?" My answer has always been, it was not me; it was God. He was able to do it because in Jesus Christ is life.

He Came So We Might Have Life

I want to express what great lengths Jesus went in order to offer you true life. Several years back, we had the opportunity to see a very powerful and moving display of Christ's death in the movie *The Passion of the Christ.* It was a painful look at what Jesus suffered for the sake of mankind. I thank God for that movie. The movie revealed God's love toward mankind, a love that is so strong that He wanted to give us a way to overcome sin and darkness. He accomplished this through the death and resurrection of Jesus, His only Son, as a sacrifice to pay o our debt to sin. Jesus came to give us life.

> "The thief cometh not, but for to steal, and to kill, and to destroy: I am come that they might have life, and that they might have it more abundantly" (John 10:10 KJV).

Jesus came and was ridiculed, mocked, betrayed, spit on, persecuted, beat beyond human recognition, and crucified so that we may have life more abundantly. This means an abundance of what life should really be, a life with our Creator. A life where He fulfills us even until eternity.

God loved us so much that He gave His only Son, and if we would believe in Him, we would not perish but have eternal life (John 3:16). Jesus sacrificed Himself and took on the sin of the world so that we could have life the way it was meant to be, both now and in eternity; but it is a choice that each of us has to make. Each person has to make an individual decision to accept Him as his or her Lord and Savior.

This is lesson is about choosing to find true life in Christ. Our path to victory must begin with Jesus Christ. For a person who does not know Jesus as Lord, true victory is not achieved. Why? The answer can be found here:

> "Therefore Jesus said again, "I tell you the truth, I am the gate for the sheep. All who ever came before me were thieves and robbers, but the sheep did not listen to them. I am the gate; whoever enters through me will be saved. He will come in and go out, and find pasture. The thief comes only to steal and kill and destroy; I have come that they may have life, and have it to the full'" (John 10:7-10).

The role of a shepherd is to lead, provide for, and take care of the sheep. The shepherd loves his sheep. Jesus explained that a true shepherd will give up His life for his sheep's well-being. However, the sheep are sometimes met with wolves and thieves who come to steal, kill, and destroy. We are the sheep, and because we are in a fallen world, some of the obstacles we have faced were because of the thief. However, Jesus is the true Shepherd of the sheep, and He came to bring us life.

Not to assume that everyone reading has made the choice to know Jesus as Lord and Savior, I want to o er the invitation to know the very Life Giver Himself. God loves you, and He has made a way for your sins to be forgiven. He wants us all to know the freedom and joy of knowing Him, of knowing what true life is like.

Most people spend their entire lives trying to live life, when in truth, we should be trying to find the One Who holds the key to true life. I thank God that He has given us the opportunity to obtain true Life.

Self-Reflection Activity

Complete the following activity and be sure to journal your thoughts.

- Read the following scriptures and consider what they mean to you: John 1:4; John 3:16–18; John 10:10.
- Ask yourself: Have I made the decision within my heart to accept Jesus Christ as my Savior and Lord?
  - If you have not and wish to do so, take the time now. Look up and read Romans 10:8 –10 and confess your sins. In your own words, pray to the Father who is willing to forgive all of your sins.
  - Turn away from the lifestyle of sin and turn toward God's way. This involves believing what the Bible says, taking to heart His scriptures and agreeing with God that His way is the right way. Now, actively search for a Bible-teaching church and begin your road to victory.
- Do you find yourself becoming absorbed with many un-fulfilling or even hurtful activities in order to fill a void in your life?
  - Make a list of current activities, relationships, and commitments.
  - Review this list and determine if any of these are getting in the way of your relationship with Christ. Keep in mind that even those who have been following Christ for many years have also found themselves occasionally distracted in their relationship with Christ.

Next Steps

Jesus said in *Matthew 10:39* "*...whoever loses his life for my sake will find it.*" One thing I have found is that when we set aside our problems and issues to serve others, in spite of what we are dealing with, we are richly blessed. Your assignment today is to perform an act of service toward someone else. It does not have to be big; the point is to give of yourself without reservation.

ONLY GOD IS TRUE LOVE

Hearing by the Word of God...

"'The Lord hath appeared of old unto me, saying, Yea, I have loved thee with an everlasting love: therefore with lovingkindness have I drawn thee'" (Jeremiah 31:3).

When I was a pre-teen, my family and I moved to a new neighborhood. This was not the first time; we had moved around quite a bit in the past. We had good reason: we needed to escape an abuser. My mom suffered physical and verbal abuse and wanted out. I was there to both hear and see what took place. Decades later, it still brings tears to my eyes. For our safety, we left quickly. Day or night, it did not matter. Sometimes we would go to shelters until we could find a new home. Moving around like this, we left behind a lot. We abandoned physical items, things of great significance, and even friendships. I got used to it. Though I was shy, I always welcomed new friends. Ironically, I think this experience enabled me to connect with a variety of people quite easily. Back to this particular move, it was significant. It seemed promising because we had moved so far away that we could not be found, at least not for several years. My mom was able to purchase a home through a program. The house was huge by my standards. My mom would go on to have a beautiful, yellow siding installed outside. The house was not in the best condition, but it was home and it was ours. With this move came new people; and at that age, I was not wise enough to distinguish their motives.

At the time, I was in an awkward stage. I was tall and skinny with a long neck and full lips. Believe me, this was not popular back then. I realize that people are now undergoing surgeries to accomplish this look, but it was not one I appreciated at the time. I was called names like giraffe and string bean. My face broke out in acne; and though my mom told me that I was pretty, I did not see it. I was also at an age when boys began to show interest in girls. While my friends were getting attention from the cute guys, I was not. Can you see where this is going?

I was the new girl on the block. The guys showed me lots of attention, more attention than I had ever experienced. My mom warned me about their motives, but I was foolish and said, "Let me learn on my own!" That was a huge mistake. Wanting to be loved, I lost my virginity not long after that. I also suffered my first heartbreak. The guy that I gave myself to connected with my "friend." I moved on, but the experience put me on a path that I would travel for almost ten years. I was in search for love.

A Strong Desire

I believe the common desire that every human being shares is the desire to be loved. This instinctive yearning does not discriminate based upon age, gender, race, or nationality. Even individuals who display a negative disposition have this desire, although it is sometimes hidden. The manifestation of this desire can be seen in the daily interactions of a newborn baby toward its parents, teenagers toward their peers, and husbands and wives toward each other. All of these natural reactions show that this is something inherent. We all have the desire to connect, the desire to be understood, the desire to be cherished and loved.

This is something that God intentionally placed within all of us. The Bible tells us in 1 John 4:8, "God is love." We crave the one thing that God is, and He uses this common thread to draw us back to Him.

"'With lovingkindness have I drawn thee'" (Jeremiah 31:3).

It can also be described as God placing a magnet inside our hearts, and He is the attracting element specifically designed to pull us into Him. People will often try to satisfy the desire to be loved with other people. The problem is that those people share that same magnet; and two magnets of the same polarity when put together repel; they do not attract. Despite their best e orts, these individuals never manage to connect because they were never designed to connect on that level. This inherent need for love is the driving force behind a variety of dysfunctional, modern relationships. The plight of the battered woman fits this profile. A woman refuses to leave her physically abusive boy-friend because she feels that she loves him, or because she thinks their relationship is what love looks like. The need to feel loved can greatly cloud our vision, and many times we seek it from those who clearly cannot provide it. Sometimes we find ourselves staying in a negative or dangerous situation in the hopes that one day that void will be filled. When left unfulfilled, emptiness can really weigh a person down. This void can never be completed by people, places, or things. Only God can flood this empty space because only God is perfect in love. If we think over the decisions that we have made in the past, we may discover that many are based upon seeking this love and trying to get it from the wrong place.

The Solution

In allowing God to draw us, we realize the intensity of His love. He loves us so much that everything He does for us is through love. Because of love, God sent Jesus and forgave us. It is by love that He protects us. It is because of love that He heals us. He even corrects us as a father does a child because He loves us.

Many people do the most damage to themselves in pursuit of something that seems hard to find: love. But true love is not hidden; it is in right in front of you. God has drawn us with a love that is everlasting. That means He will never tell you that He does not love you anymore. You can count on His love for you to remain. The greatest thing in life is to finally find the One to fulfill the desire that we have been longing for, and that someone is God.

When I found God's love, it caused such a change in me that I never wanted to turn back. I learned that it is not possible to find what I was looking for in a person. Does that mean my desire to marry was gone? Not at all. What it meant was I finally stopped looking in the wrong places. I realized that God is love (See 1 John 4:8). There is no one who can love me or fulfill me more than Him. Because He is love, love is only perfected in Him. I realize now that people make mistakes, and though they may love us, they cannot be perfect. This kind of love caused me to go from being bitter and angry to finding joy and gladness. My heavy heart was lifted. I was so drastically changed that people noticed my transformation. My attitude, my way of thinking, and what I said no longer shouted, "BITTER!" I had been drawn by true love, and so can you.

In the previous lesson, we read that the True Shepherd loves the sheep. We also learned that one of the roles of the shepherd is to lead the sheep. You are one of His sheep and He loves you. God draws you toward Himself because of this love. Be assured that His desire for you is good, therefore He will constantly lead you in your path. Understanding that God loves you and wants the best for you will allow you to trust that He will lead you on this road. When met with obstacles in your path, rely upon the love of the Shepherd Who will lead you even through the difficulties.

Now Carriers of Love

Once we find true love, we can love God and love our neighbors. We can live out a life of love.

"Be imitators of God, therefore, as dearly loved children and live a life of love..." (Ephesians 5:1–2).

Our mission as Christians is to display the love of God openly; and to accomplish this we need a relationship with God the Father, Jesus Christ His Son, and the promised Holy Spirit, Who abides within the heart of the believer. People are naturally drawn to love, so it is only fitting that we find ourselves drawn to the Possessor of that love. At this point we not only hold the magnet (desire) but also the attracting element (love of God).

Self-Reflection Activity

Complete the following activity and be sure to journal your thoughts.

- Read the following scriptures and consider what they mean to you: Jeremiah 31:3; Ephesians 3:16–19; Ephesians 5:1-2.
- Do you truly accept the love that God has for you?
- As a Christian, are you able to display the same love that God shows for you toward others, even those to whom you feel do not deserve it?

Next Steps

Jeremiah 31:3 reads, "The LORD hath appeared of old unto me, saying, Yea, I have loved thee with an everlasting love: therefore with loving kindness have I drawn thee." After having great challenges in the area of love, sometimes it is hard to understand why a holy God would love us. Today, remind yourself often of His love by reflecting on this scripture. Also make a list of the people who are more of a challenge to love. Begin praying for them, showing them kindness in spite of this challenge; and ask God to give you the ability to love them unconditionally. When we think of how undeserving we are of God's love, it can help us to love those who we feel are undeserving of ours.

LET GO OF SHAME

Hearing by the Word of God...

"Anyone who believes in him will never be put to shame" (Romans 10:11-13).

Shame is something carried deeply inside. It eats away at a person like decay. Personal experience with it has made me well-acquainted with its tactics. It suggests that you have committed the ultimate wrong. It makes you feel like you are the only one in the situation. Then it makes you wear an invisible label that shouts, "I am unworthy!" It causes you to hang your head low. It holds such a grasp on its victims that it seems unescapable. I am no stranger to its unbearable grip. I have been stricken by the mere thought of others knowing my indiscretions. Over the years, I have done things that left me feeling deeply ashamed. One incident of great significance happened many years ago. To my regret, I had an abortion.

I was young, still in high school, and I did not want to disappoint. However I was ultimately to blame. While lying there clothed in a shabby hospital gown in what seemed to be the whitest and brightest clinic ever, the regrets started to amount. Even before the procedure began, tears made their way down my cheeks. Then they came more quickly, like a constant flow. I was about to abort my baby.

I wanted to get up and run, even with my back side exposed! Nonetheless, the nurse was nice and comforting; but the person issuing the procedure showed no visible signs of emotions. I can still picture all of the machines surrounding me. I watched the whole thing, although I do not know why. Maybe I felt the need to face what I was doing. I saw the tubing that extracted the baby. Though what I saw no longer resembled human life, that is exactly how it started. It was such a high power machine, the baby never had a chance.

It was such a painful experience, not physically but emotionally. Immediately following the procedure, I was allowed to put on my clothes and go to a room full of reclining chairs. There were other people there that faced the same misfortune. They gave us all blankets to keep us warm. We were also given graham crackers and juice. I just sat there with so many things running through my mind. I knew what I did was a big deal, and I carried the guilt for many years. I told only a few people. More than ten years had passed. The memory had been suppressed. Then I found my Savior and was born anew.

New Creatures in Christ

The Bible says that we have become new people in Christ. The person that we were previously has passed on (see 2 Corinthians 5:17). To be exact, it says we are new creatures, which is a much more descriptive picture. In our old way of life, prior to the submission to God, we chose to bow to sin instead of God. Now that we are in Christ, those old ways have passed and the newness of being the children of God has come into our lives. At this time, we received a renewed spirit. As we renew our minds with God's Word, we begin to think di erently; even our values change.

At the beginning of my rededication to Christ, things were wonderful; I knew that I was different. I was on a natural high, and it seemed no one could bring me down. But slowly, memories of the past started creeping back. Friends would jokingly say to me, "I remember the old Nicole." They meant no harm and appreciated the change, but the seeds of the past were still being planted. At this point, I had befriended several women who loved God. Many of them had committed their lives to Him at a young age. I assumed they stayed out of trouble the whole time. Of course, I felt I was the "more experienced" in the bunch. Ironically, it seemed like these former inadequacies found this new place in my life. Memories of the past came to mind again. Shameful consequences reared their heads. I became consumed with my past that it almost controlled me and stopped me from living out my new Christian identity.

Accepting the Truth

I finally found the courage to tell a friend what I was experiencing. Having witnessed me crumble as a result of the shame, she told me that God could heal me emotionally. At first I thought, *There is nothing emotionally wrong with me.* It took me a couple of years to realize that she was right and that shame was keeping me in bondage. When I finally came to grips with it, I knew I had to allow God to do His work. Previously, I was not allowing Him to do what He wanted to do for me, which was to free me. I had not accepted that I was a new creature in Christ; but now it was time. Let's take a closer look:

> "For the love of Christ compels us, because we judge thus: that if One died for all, then all died; and He died for all, that those who live should live no longer for themselves, but for Him who died for them and rose again.
>
> Therefore, from now on, we regard no one according to the flesh. Even though we have known Christ according to the flesh, yet now we know Him thus no longer. Therefore, if anyone is in Christ, he is a new creation; old things have passed away; behold, all things have become new" (2 Corinthians 5:14-17 NKJV).

According to this passage, anyone who is in Christ is a new creation. That is a big deal! "New creation" means something that did not previously exist. According to the above passage, if I am in Christ, then this applies to me! Many times, it is hard to accept this scripture for ourselves. Who you were before is no longer the person you are now. You are newly-formed because of Christ. Is this still hard to grasp?

One of the best examples and vivid pictures of this concept of the new creation is in that of the life cycle of a caterpillar. Like the born-again believer, the caterpillar starts off in a totally different state from its final condition. It goes through a process of change. Its end result is much different from its beginning. By the end of the process, it has grown beautifully-colored wings and now flies! It is indeed a miracle, the same miracle that happens when we are in Christ. Accepting this allowed me to submit my shame to God. My acceptance was not overnight, but in due time it became my truth.

His Good Purposes

Once I submitted my shame to Him, I was overwhelmed with a freedom that I cannot explain. I no longer spent time wondering what would people think of me; and I also realized that when God healed me emotionally, it opened many opportunities for me.

He showed me that what I thought would be detrimental to my journey actually turned out to be for His glory. For years I had carried this weight, making me believe that I was an outcast; but what I learned was that for those who love the Lord and are called by His name, all things work together for their good and His good purpose (Romans 8:28).

After recognizing the need for freedom and ridding my life of shame, I could now carry out God's work in my life. This is why freedom from shame is so important; it allows us to liberally share our stories. We should never be ashamed of our pasts because it is what God can use to display His Power here on earth; we can reveal His unfailing love so that others can know that *"...where the Spirit of the Lord is, there is liberty" (2 Corinthians 3:17 KJV)*.

A Caution to You

I know that we are on a journey, but there are certain things we cannot take along. One thing I know is that women are good at carrying baggage, and shame is likely the heaviest load. If you are still carrying any degree of shame, I want to encourage you to put it down. You can cast this care upon Jesus and leave it with Him (1 Peter 5:7). Jesus has freed you, so He is not the one keeping you bound to past sin and shame. The road to victory is ahead of you as long as you are following Christ. However, your travels will be made easier if you accept the freedom you have been given. Do not let shame be an obstacle that you have the power to remove. Be empowered to believe that Jesus has set you free from shame.

Self-Reflection Activity

Complete the following activity and be sure to journal your thoughts.

- Read the following scriptures and consider what they mean to you: 2 Corinthians 5:17; Romans 10:11–13.
- Is there an area of bondage in your life that is hindering your walk with Christ?
- Is this bondage, whether shame or something else, hindering you from fulfilling God's purpose in your life? Make a list of these areas of shame or bondage.

Next Steps

1 Peter 5:8 reads, "Be self–controlled and alert. Your enemy the devil prowls around like a roaring lion looking for someone to devour." One of the ways that Satan stands between us and God is by keeping people in bondage and shame. He taunts us and reminds us of past sins in an attempt to paralyze us. The Bible tells us in 2 Corinthians 10:5 that we can capture those thoughts and make them subject to Christ. Take the list that you created in the activity above and present them to God. Then, as you are reminded of them, arrest the thought and profess the freedom that Christ gave you. *"It is for freedom that Christ has set us free" (Galatians 5:1).*

LESSON FOUR

THERE IS REST
FOR THE WEARY

Hearing by the Word of God...

"He who dwells in the shelter of the Most High will rest in the shadow of the Almighty" (Psalms 91:1).

When I was twenty-seven-years-old, I purchased my first home. The house was small for the most part. I was still single with no children, so it was more than enough space for me. I was excited. The house was beautiful by my standards. It was well-maintained by the previous owners. The design was that of a bungalow style frame with a brick exterior. The attic had been converted into a bedroom with an additional area, usable as a small office or play area for children. The basement was also updated to include an additional area for entertaining guests. Still being single, I had to learn how to maintain and care for the lawn. I did pretty well, I might add. I enjoyed my new home.

Then one summer, a neighbor invited summer guests, a couple of nieces from out of state. These were "new girls on the block." It was not long before I started to notice heavy traffic

27

around their house. Young men were certainly interested in them. They sat outside well into the night, which was no problem. I remember being young and sitting out on the porch with friends after dark. However, the company that visited these young ladies were not respectful to the neighbors. They parked at the house and played loud music. There was enough bass to cause my heart to pound. I guess they wanted to impress the young ladies. However, I did not appreciate being awakened at odd times of the night to the sound of my windows rattling. As a woman living in a house alone, it was likely not wise for me to approach the perpetrators. But I could not resist, and I spoke to at least one of the visitors about the noise level. He was very respectful and obliging to my request to turn the music down. When the summer ended, the young ladies left. All was well again, at least that was what I thought.

During this time, the neighborhood changed. I began noticing excessive tra c and illegal activity overrunning my neighborhood. I became aware of home invasions of which I was also a victim; these happenings raised certain safety concerns. I spoke to someone about this, and she told me of the same type of problems she had experienced in the past. She went on to remind me of the ninety-first Psalm.

Dwelling in God's Presence

This particular passage of scripture describes the protection of God for His people, those who abide in the Presence of God. These are those who heed God's command to draw near to Him. They come to God, not in word but from their heart. They find themselves earnestly and wholeheartedly seeking

Him. These people want to be close to God as much as they can, to dwell in His "secret place." For a period of time, I began reading and reflecting on this scripture every day. Each time I did this, something different seemed to reveal itself.

A Place of Rest

Initially, the protection I focused on was physical protection; but then the Word began to reveal to me the spiritual protection that God has for His people. I realized that the shield of God covers every part of me, and then allows me to rest in Him.

The writer of Psalm 91 metaphorically describes God's "secret place" as a place of refuge, a place of protection, a place where no enemy can go, a place where we can run and hide. This is a place where we can dwell in the Presence of God. Darkness cannot dwell here. And because we know this, we can rest completely from the fear of danger and our enemy.

Because the writer of Psalm 91 knows that dwelling in the presence of God means living under His protection, he is able to say:

> "You will not fear the terror of night, nor the arrow that flies by day, nor the pestilence that stalks in the darkness, nor the plague that destroys at midday. A thousand may fall at your side, ten thousand at your right hand, but it will not come near you" (Psalms 91:5–7).

The Shield of Faithfulness

We face many mental challenges each day that come specifically to test our faith. These come with the intention of causing doubt and fear; yet, the passage we just read tells us not to be anxious about these realities. It essentially says, "It may look like it is coming at me, but because of the protection of God, it will never even touch me." He says in Psalm 91:4 *"...His faithfulness will be your shield and rampart."* The shield of faithfulness is protecting us from every arrow of the enemy, every trick, every trap, and every way the enemy tries to harm us; therefore, we can fully trust God.

Accept His Secure Rest

This security belongs to those who:

> *"Make the Most High your dwelling—even the LORD, who is my refuge" and because of this "then no harm will befall you, no disaster will come near your tent. For he will command his angels concerning you to guard you in all your ways; they will lift you up in their hands, so that you will not strike your foot against a stone" (Psalm 91:9–12).*

When we entered the Kingdom of God and began seeking Him, He gave us rest. Our God gave us rest from everything we ever feared, namely the fear of attack by our enemies. In order to experience this, we must draw near to Him. Attaining this peace means we have to come to the reality that He gave us this rest. Once we understand what dwelling in this place means, we have peace. When those arrows come near, those threats,

those negative thoughts, those feelings of "what if this happens" or "what if I fail," always remember that He has given you
rest. You no longer have reason to fear.

Rest Is Needed on Your Journey

The road to victory is one we will travel our entire lives.
This is because our destination is eternity with Christ. This
means that the journey may be long. It will need to be travelled
at a steady pace. At the same time, the obstacles will still arise
from time to time. For your journey, you will need to make sure
that you draw near to God. In that "secret place," you will find
both rest and protection. Because of God's faithfulness, you can
take a break and let Him handle the "arrows, tricks, and traps of
the enemy." He is more than equipped to do it. Allow yourself
the rest that God provides in His secret place. Just as the children of Israel, you will also be able to exclaim: *"... we sought him
and he has given us rest on every side..." (Chronicles 14:7b).*

Self-Reflection Activity

Complete the following activity and be sure to journal your thoughts.

- Read the following scriptures and consider what they mean to you: Psalm 91 & Mark 4:37–40.
- Are there personal fears keeping you from the rest that God intended for you?
- Are you able to recognize God's presence in your life on a daily basis? If so, because of this reality, are you assured of His protection?

Next Steps

Psalms 91:1 reads, "He who dwells in the shelter of the Most High will rest in the shadow of the Almighty." Start setting aside time to spend in daily prayer, worship, meditation, and/or study. This should be done in a quiet place with just you and God. Begin with small increments of time, maybe fifteen minutes. You will find that you will begin to crave this time; and before you know it, you will have no problem spending hours with Jesus. For your initial e ort, take a month and begin a daily confession of Psalm 91, rehearsing the verses and pondering its meaning.

WORRYING HINDERS GROWTH

Hearing by the Word of God...

"But the worries of this life, the deceitfulness of wealth and the desires for other things come in and choke the word, making it unfruitful" (Mark 4:19).

My mother has been my biggest cheerleader for my entire life. She encouraged me in my academics. She praised me for my achievements. She even supported whatever obscure ideas I dared to follow. I think the positive role she played encouraged me to do "big things." Despite humble beginnings, I attended college and pursued a promising career. After earning a degree, I secured a job at a top technology company. This was new territory. Sure, I was nervous, but excited as well. My future looked promising.

All was well until one day my co-workers and I arrived at work to find that quite a few people were met with exit letters and empty boxes on their desks. I was mortified. Though I had worked in office settings much of my collegiate career, I had never witnessed such a thing. The company made significant cut backs, laying off people without warning. They had to leave their long-time co-workers and friends at a moment's notice. Though I was not included in these cuts, my first inclination was, "This could happen to me."

The nature of the technology industry is one where people work long hours, sacrifice family time, and are called on in the middle of the night. This is without overtime pay. The pay is decent, but the work can be taxing. Some of the same people who were being exited out of the door were seen previously toiling away well into the late evenings and nights. This incident triggered a thought in me: job security did not exist for anyone. In all the time and money I spent in college, no one ever mentioned anything like this. I was not prepared. My co-workers had "the rug" pulled from underneath them, and I did not want that to happen to me. I was immensely discouraged and began to worry about my job stability. Did you hear me? I began to worry.

God's Word Unapplied

This incident opened a door that I willingly walked through. In hindsight, I wished I had not allowed myself to take that path; but I found more and more reasons to worry even after learning what the Bible says about anxiety. One day, I had to ask myself, "Why is it that I know the Word of God, but sometimes when challenges occur, I forget what the Word says?" It seems like in these times, I have forgotten God's promises as they related to my situation. Instead of applying the promises of God, I panicked. A former pastor explained the difference between wisdom and knowledge. He said that wisdom is the ability to apply what you know. It is amazing that we   can know what to do in a situation, yet we choose not to do it.

Restricting God's Word

If we let our worries overpower our faith in God, we do not give the Word of God the opportunity to produce God's truth in our lives. Here, the Word is not doing us any good because instead of applying it, we are worrying. Ever wonder why Jesus said:

> *"So do not worry, saying, 'What shall we eat?' or 'What shall we drink?' or 'What shall we wear?'... Your heavenly Father knows that you need them. But seek first his kingdom and his righteousness, and all these things will be given to you as well" (Matthew 6:31–33).*

Sometimes we allow our focus to change during times of adversity and unexpected challenges. When we worry, the tendency to first seek God's direction goes out the window. To make matters worse, we often become angry about our situation, and the inclination to seek Him first is likely nonexistent. We suddenly feel like *we* have to fix the problem or react to the situation and forego seeking God. We barely give Him a chance to reveal the solution.

Seeking God for Our Situation

The funny thing is that in the end, after we have done what we thought we should do and it does not work, then we go to God. This is when we begin to seek Him and apply what we have learned in His Word. At this time, things either work out or God gives us peace in the matter. We later realize that we could have saved ourselves a headache or two by doing this from the beginning. However, there are times when we do not even make an effort to handle the matter in a godly manner, and we wonder why the Word is not working for us.

Above All We Can Think

Jesus told us not to worry because He knew the heart of man. Jesus knew that we would worry about everything. Jesus knew that there was really no need to worry because as it is written, He

> *"Is able to do exceeding abundantly above all that we ask or think, according to the power that worketh in us" (Ephesians 3:20 KJV).*

Jesus gave us the solution, which is to seek God first and His righteousness.

The State of God's Word in My Heart

The parable of the sower adequately reveals the nature of our hearts in regards to God's Word (see Mark 4:1-20). Jesus talks about a farmer sowing seed. The seed does not always make it to its proper place. He explained that some fell along the path, some among rocks, some among thorns, and finally some on good soil. The only seed that actually produced a return was that which was sown on the good soil. He explained that this mirrored the state of our heart towards the Word. In my case, my worry revealed that I might not have been the one who had "seed sown on good soil" (Mark 4:20). Unfortunately, my heart closely resembled the soil where the Word was sown among the thorns of my life. I allowed the cares of this world to choke the Word, which is why I sometimes had trouble applying the Word of God to unexpected situations.

So I had to ask myself, "How do I allow my seed to be 'sown on good soil' and to 'produce a crop?'" The answer: My heart must become "good soil."

Heart Preparation

Good soil is that which has been prepared, broken up, and processed until it is capable of allowing the seed to settle into itself. Good soil is no longer hard and resistant; it is the type of soil where thorns cannot grow.

Our hearts are like the soil, and if our hearts are hardened and resistant, then we are not teachable. If we are not teachable, then the Word cannot be planted properly within us. If the Word cannot be properly planted, then the worries and cares of this life become greater than our desire to seek God. When we do not seek God first, we cannot produce a crop based on the Word; instead, the Word is unfruitful in our lives.

David as Our Example

David, the king of Israel, is a great example of a man who sought after God. Each time David inquired of God for direction, David was successful. David could have let the threat of countless enemies overwhelm him; but instead, he sought God. God not only gave him instruction, but God also strengthened him in the midst of his fear. We have to make sure we never allow the cares of this life to harden our hearts towards the Word. We have to make sure that we always have a reverential fear of God. We have to make sure that in spite of all, no matter what, we must "...seek ye first the kingdom of God" (Matthew 6:33 KJV). We must always remember that the Word sown on "good soil" will always produce a crop.

Free Yourself from Worry

I want to encourage you that worry is not something that you want to take along for the ride. It will hinder your growth and ability to deal with any hurdles you may face. You have been equipped with a very powerful tool, and that is the Word of God. However, as we saw, the word you receive is restricted because of worry. I mention this because the Word of God contains wisdom, knowledge, and instruction. You will need all of this for your earthly travels. Christ is leading you to victory, and He has said there is no gain in worrying. But you can trust that God will take care of you (Matthew 6:27-30). With that said, please free yourself of all anxiety by casting your cares upon Him, because He does care for you.

Self-Reflection Activity

Complete the following activity and be sure to journal your thoughts.

- Read the following scriptures and consider what they mean to you: Mark 4:1-20.
- Do you find yourself worrying about things you can do nothing about?
- When problems arise in your life, do you go to God for direction and comfort, or do you try to solve things on your own?

Next Steps

Matthew 6:25–26 reads, "Therefore I tell you, do not worry about your life, what you will eat or drink; or about your body, what you will wear. Is not life more important than food, and the body more important than clothes? Look at the birds of the air; they do not sow or reap or store away in barns, and yet your heavenly Father feeds them. Are you not much more valuable than they?" Begin to make this confession: "If He takes care of the birds and the lilies, surely, He will take care of me."

HOPE ANCHORS THE SOUL

Hearing by the Word of God...

"...We might have strong consolation, who have fled for refuge to lay hold of the hope set before us. This hope we have as an anchor of the soul, both sure and steadfast, and which enters the Presence behind the veil, where the forerunner has entered for us, even Jesus, having become High Priest forever according to the order of Melchizedek"
(Hebrews 6:18-20 NKJV).

I married at a time in my life that I would consider to be rather late. I was thirty-two years of age. For as far back as I could remember, I wanted to have children. My husband and I waited about a year before expanding our family. Month after month, I grew increasingly discouraged because I had not conceived. We tried several methods, like counting days and taking my temperature; but nothing happened. I even took early-detecting pregnancy tests each month. One day, I tested, and to my excitement, there were two lines! My husband was also excited, and despite my request to keep it between ourselves, he could not contain himself.

I could not believe it. Finally, my chance to be a Mommy and to love on a little person. It was a dream come true. A few days after the great news, I started experiencing signs of a menstrual cycle. *Not a big deal*, I thought. Then I became concerned when the flow seemed to be like a normal cycle. I called the doctor, and an immediate appointment was set up. Upon my arrival, I saw an ultrasound technician first. She began asking questions that concerned me. Then said, "I don't see signs of pregnancy."

"But I saw the tests and I took more than one," I frantically exclaimed. She reassured me that not only did she see no signs of me being pregnant, but she did not see signs that I had been pregnant and miscarried. My heart sank. I did not understand. What could have gone wrong? After speaking with the doctor, she decided to perform a blood test. Later, the test revealed that I was in fact pregnant. We had conceived. But the news only grew worse.

The doctor asked if the test indicators were faint. I told her they were, but why did that matter? She explained to me that I had experienced what is called chemical pregnancy, a term that I had not heard before. This is a condition when the man's sperm successfully penetrates the woman's egg, but the fertilized egg never attaches to the uterus. She said it happens often, and most women do not realize it; they think their menstrual cycle has started late. She also cautioned us not to try again for a while because my hormones were "out of whack." When we left, my mind began to fill with many thoughts of doubts and insecurities. I questioned whether or not my abortion caused this trauma. I decided I did not want to try anymore because I lost all hope.

Hope Implies the Need for Dependence

In today's society, we have become so independent that we are accustomed to handling almost everything ourselves. There is a vast amount of information at our disposal, much more than what we have had in the past. We are able to make decisions and put our plans into action to obtain our goals. The very thought of relying on someone else eats away at our pride. It is as if we have become so technologically advanced that we think we know everything. There comes a time when we find that there are some things beyond our control or ability to handle. As you read, the pregnancy experience taught me this first hand.

A Limited Sphere of Influence

Every now and then, there are situations that become barriers, blocking the road to our plans. We have done everything we can and know how to do, even calling others that we think can help, but nothing happens. When you reach this point, this edge of sanity, where is your hope? The question is assuming that you are still holding onto some sort of optimism. In situations that we can resolve, our hope is either in ourselves, our abilities, or the abilities of others. What do we do when we get to a place where everyone's hands are tied? Do we still have hope, and if so, in whom is our hope found?

Let's face it: Life's situations have a way of raining on our parades. When this happens, we hit that wall and we may feel discouraged. My reaction to the news about the pregnancy was to shut down. I felt like there was nothing I could do. This was out of my hands. Why even try? My husband was the one who convinced me not to give up. He encouraged me out of the slump of hopelessness. Thank God for him. I am not sure how long I would have stayed in that place if he did not allow God to use him to encourage me.

Rebuilding Hope

Undesirable situations happen to everyone, some more harshly than others. I have personally heard of people enduring circumstances like receiving news of infertility, experiencing a life-altering injury, being let go from a job in a failing economy, being diagnosed with an incurable disease, or experiencing a failing marriage. All of these situations are beyond our control. Faced with such situations, we feel like all hope is gone. This is a hard place to be. But what should you do? There is One called Jesus Christ who has no limits. We must rebuild our hope in Him. This is the hope in which our souls can hold secure.

What is your situation? Have you faced something that has left you hopeless? If so, let's do something about it because hope is what will anchor your soul in troubling situations. It is what will keep you from running away and giving up.

> *"This hope we have as an anchor of the soul, both sure and steadfast"* *(Hebrews 6:19).*

In my case, I needed to rebuild my hope in Christ. I had remembered being taught to find a scripture and "stand" on the truth of that scripture. I found the following verse:

"But did He not make them one, having a remnant of the Spirit? And why one? He seeks godly offspring" (Malachi 2:15 NKJV).

I repeated this scripture as often as possible. I needed to remind myself that God wants us to raise up godly children to fill the earth. I remember having a dream in which I held a baby. I felt impressed in my heart that I would be a mother, and that reassured me. I believe these were His gentle ways of showing that He loves me; and guess what? We did go on to get pregnant a month later!

The Impossible Happened

When I called the doctor, she did not believe it. She was convinced the test was falsely positive or that my urine was causing the positive because of the chemical pregnancy. But I knew better. I had taken at least three tests this time, and the colors were nice and bright. I had to convince her to draw my blood again, and she finally agreed. The test showed my hormones levels were higher than the previous conception. I was surely pregnant! My God did it! My hope beyond hope caused the impossible to happen. You know what? I get to see the tangible evidence of God's power every time I look at our son.

The Anchor for Your Soul

As long as we live, something will happen that puts us in uncontrollable situations. What will you do the next time it happens or even if it is happening now? In whom will you place your hope?

> *"This hope we have as an anchor of the soul, both sure and steadfast"* (Hebrews 6:19).

I like the imagery that comes to mind when I think of hope as an anchor for the soul. I picture it holding everything in place. You will only drift so far when anchored. Discouragement is sure to meet you along the way, but the hope you have in Christ can keep you securely on your path. When faced with obstacles, let it be a reminder to keep your hope in Christ; it will be the security for your soul.

Self-Reflection Activity

Complete the following activity and be sure to journal your thoughts.

- Read the following scriptures and consider what they mean to you: Mark 10:27; Colossians 1:27
- When you are stuck in a situation, who do you usually turn to?
- Do you still have hope that God can do something about even the most trying situation in your life?

Next Steps

Ephesians 2:12–13 reads, "Remember that at that time you were separate from Christ, excluded from citizenship in Israel and foreigners to the covenants of the promise, without hope and without God in the world. But now in Christ Jesus you who once were far away have been brought near through the blood of Christ." When Jesus Christ died and rose, He brought hope of salvation to those who would accept Him. Today's activity is to reflect on this scripture and ponder what it means to you personally. Let this passage bring encouragement and hope to you.

OUR GOD IS FAITHFUL

Hearing by the Word of God...

"Moreover David said, 'The Lord, who delivered me from the paw of the lion and from the paw of the bear, He will deliver me from the hand of this Philistine'"(1 Samuel 17:37 NJKV).

When my husband and I met and married, the agreement was that I would move to New York in December of that year. I was really concerned about selling my house, which didn't look so promising. My house lost value, and I bordered on needing to pay out money to my mortgage company after closing. I put a sign in the front yard that read, "For Sale by Owner." As it would happen, I did find a buyer. I made a deal with my agent and he only charged me a small fee to list the house. He also secured representation for the buyer. He explained my situation and they understood. As things would have it, I was expected to come out even. This was great!

Things with my job were also working out well. I was able to keep my position and work from home. It seemed that all was lining up in my favor. Back then, the mortgaging process seemed to take an eternity, but we were given an estimated closing date that worked within our schedule. The buyer's

funding process was not moving as quickly as we initially expected. Time passed, and we had no solid date to close on the
house. I became really nervous.

The week of my relocation arrived, and my husband prepared to travel to Michigan in order to drive me and my belongings back to New York. I only had one minor issue: My
house had not been officially sold! For about a month, I had
anxiously awaited the news of a closing date, but to no avail.
That week, I finally "threw up my hands" and said, "I'm moving
anyway." I packed up my house, got rid of furniture, and con-
solidated my belongings to only what would fit inside my
Grand Prix. This was one of the biggest leaps of faith I have
taken to date. I left a friend with the power of attorney; and the
day after Christmas, we packed the car and headed to NYC. A
few days later, I received news that the closing date was set: December 30th. Hallelujah! My God was faithful to bring this to
pass.

David: An Example of Preparation

King David was one of the most favorable people written
about in the Bible. He was fearless and bold; a warrior and a
conqueror. David also had a heart for God, was a servant of
God, and sought God earnestly. David was not perfect. In fact,
he committed several shocking sins; but he loved God so much
that he repented of his sin. He never wanted God to take away
the comfort of His Spirit.

Prior to becoming king of Israel, God chose and anointed
David. The Bible says that after David was anointed by Samuel,
from that day on, the Spirit of the Lord came on him in power

(1 Samuel 16:13). I would like to point out that the Spirit of the Lord came upon David after he was anointed. I believe God had Samuel anoint David to endow him with power to prepare him for his coming role as king.

After this time, David did not immediately take on this role; he went back to shepherding sheep. While still a shepherd boy, he would later fight Goliath and become a hero. During David's tenure as a shepherd, he met opposition that tried to attack his flock. Being a good shepherd, David stood up against this opposition; and because the Spirit of the Lord was upon him, he had the power to overcome his foe. Therefore, as we fast forward to the story of David and Goliath, we can see why he had great courage.

Remembering God's Faithfulness

When David fought Goliath, David confidently destroyed the giant because he reflected on what God had previously done for him. He remembered his fight with the lion and the bear. Can you imagine fighting a lion? A big, overpowering beast with an imposing mouth of large teeth, used to rip apart its prey? The Bible says that the lion is "...mighty among beasts" and "retreats before nothing" (Proverbs 30:30). It is safe to say that this lion was probably not afraid of David and met him with the same fierceness as all other foes.

I think many times we hear or read the story about David and Goliath and never look at the significance of fighting a lion or bear. Many of us have heard this story from our youth, so we tend to take it for granted. One day as I read this, it dawned on me just how powerful lions and bears can be. Yet,

God fought for David in both of these instances, and David's life was spared. God beat those enemies for David, and it would not be the last time.

When David heard Goliath taunting the army, it meant nothing to him to stand up to the giant. He saw Goliath in the same way that he saw the lion and the bear. He knew that God's power was with him.

A Wall of Remembrance

When we have our own giants, trials, persecutions, or struggles, we are able, like David, to file away those memories of how God delivered us safely. We have to build our wall with stones of God's faithfulness. Based on those memories, we are able to say just what David said: "...this uncircumcised Philistine will be like one of them..." (1 Samuel 17:36). We have to recognize the work of God in our lives, however small we think it is. We have been given the promise from God that no weapon will be allowed to prosper against the children of the Lord; this is our heritage (Isaiah 54:17). Therefore, like David, we can come before our enemy in every situation in full assurance that the battle is won because the battle belongs to the Lord. We have to be continuously aware that our God is with us and recognize that His Spirit lives in us. Moreover, since His Spirit is alive in us, we have power, and eventually we should come to realize the complete confidence to know that just as He did it before, He will do it again.

He Did It Again!

I like to recall memories of God's faithfulness to me. This recollection acts as a faith booster. When that house sold at the very end of the year, I knew God had done it. He is faithful like that. History would seem to repeat itself. My husband and I were met with the same challenge again. We purchased our first home together, and a year later, America experienced the housing-market crash. Our house loss value, and again our mortgage was more than the house was worth. We wanted to move to another location, and for years we thought we had no choice but to stay; and we did remain there for eight years. We did not consider God's faithfulness. We finally decided to put our house on the market. My husband prayed a very specific prayer, and together we kept going before God. And God did it again. We not only had multiple offers, but they were higher than our asking price.

Cling to Your "God Moments"

The path to victory is best travelled while remembering God's faithfulness. As you know, the road of life can be a little bumpy. During these times, you need to know that God will work things out. You can prepare yourself ahead of time by recording your "God moments." What is a "God moment?" It is a time when God has worked things out for your good. You want these for future reference, especially as you go through rough patches. Keeping these as reminders can serve as an encouragement to you. I want you to know within your heart that our God is faithful.

Self-Reflection Activity

Complete the following activity and be sure to journal your thoughts.

- Read the following scriptures and consider what they mean to you: 1 Samuel 17:25–37.
- What giants has God defeated for you in the past?
- When di erent giants arise in your life, do you rest assured that God will come through like always?
- If not, what steps can you take to actively come to this assurance?

Next Steps

When the children of Israel crossed the Jordan River into the land of Canaan, the LORD instructed them to set up stones to remind them that He brought them into the Promised Land. Likewise, we should set up reminders of God's great work in our lives so that in trying times, we can remember how He delivered us previously. For today's assignment, make a list of times when God came to your rescue. Thank Him for each time He has come through for you, and keep this list handy for future reference.

A CHANGE IN PERSPECTIVE CHANGES EVERYTHING

Hearing by the Word of God...

"And there we saw the giants... and we were in our own sight as grasshoppers, and so we were in their sight" (Numbers 13:33 KJV).

As I mentioned previously, I relocated to New York City after marrying my husband. One day while working at home, I experienced the worst cramps ever! This pain was so severe, it brought me to my knees. I did not know what was going on, so I called my husband and he rushed home from work. He made sure I was okay; and after that day, I was fine. This turned out to be one incident, never to occur again. A few months later, we moved to Dallas and I started having really sharp pains in my side. These were not the same type of pains, but it seemed weird that I had begun having these sort of issues. I finally saw a doctor, and after a sonogram, I learned the pain was caused by a nickel sized ovarian cyst.

I do not know if you realize this but when a person already has a tendency to worry, receiving news of a cyst is not good. Hearing a doctor say that cysts are common meant nothing to me. We inquired about the options to remove it, one of them being birth control pills. Since I had previous issues with this type of medication, this was not an option for us, so we refused. This situation was huge.

An Example of Broadened Perspective

During a weekly meeting at work, our boss presented a video that portrayed two views of life with Earth being the center of each. The beginning took us on a journey to the streets of Italy where we watched street performers entertain the crowd. The radius expanded so that the people and the street appeared smaller and we were able to view more of the city. The range continued to increase until we found ourselves viewing the earth from space; it was about the size of a basketball and took up most of the picture, but we could no longer see the details of the city. Our view continued to expand; we saw the earth, the sun, moon, stars, and other planets within the same solar system. From this view, we were able to see where the earth sat in relation to other planets surrounding it; and at this point it looked to be the size of a golf ball.

As our view was widened, we found that there are millions of galaxies in the universe. The view of the earth at this point was almost unnoticeable, probably the same size of a speck. This is what some people refer to as seeing the "big picture."

An Example of Focused Perspective

The next part of the video was just the opposite. Instead of expanding the view, it became more focused. This portion allowed us to look at a drop of water under a microscope where we found that a world of organisms lived in a single drop of water. Here, our view continued to focus until we got to see what we know right now to be the smallest particles of matter: the atom. This kind of perspective can be referred to as "tunnel vision."

The purpose of this video was for us to understand our perspective as it relates to our job activities. And this became a great learning tool for me in my personal life.

Our Vantage Point

Perspective can be understood as the point of view. When we are looking at an object, we not only see the object, but we also realize its position and distance from where we stand, thus our perspective. Perspective is personal, which is why people respond to things differently. No one can share your same viewpoint because they cannot occupy your current position. How we view and act upon things tend to be related to our inner perspective. Since perspective relates to focus and positioning, we can note that our interpretation of what we are viewing can change when we alter our vantage point. Since this book is about victory over obstacles, let's take a look at perspective in terms of our circumstances.

Perspective in Relation to Circumstances

When a problem presents itself, what is your normal perspective on it? Do you lean toward seeing it in a broadened form? Do you tend to focus in on your issue? When we focus closely on ourselves, everything that affects us seems bigger. On the contrary, when we make ourselves smaller and focus on more important facets of our lives, everything that affects us seems smaller. A problem can be handled differently in both perspectives, and we see this in God's initial attempt to lead Israel into the land of Canaan.

To give a brief summary, God had promised the Israelites some land, and sent twelve men to explore it. When they went out, they saw that the land was as God said. The land was very fertile and more than adequate for living. The problem arose when they also saw many giants. Ten of the twelve men lost their confidence, and only two were willing to take the land. What hindered the ten were not the giants, but their perspective of the giants.

Our Trials in Perspective to God

How or where do we set our perspective? There are many ways, but I am only going to mention a few. We can focus on the smallest elements of ourselves. We can look at things from a social point of view. We can look at things from the world's viewpoint. Or we can expand our perspective to the most expansive point of view, through the eyes of God.

Caleb and Joshua measured themselves and their problem through God's perspective. We know that God is: all seeing

(Psalm 33:13), all knowing (Psalm 147:5), all powerful (Job 42:2), and everywhere (Psalm 139:7), which makes Him superior to all.

To the ten spies, the people looked like giants; but to the giants, God is enormous. Sometimes challenges attempt to overwhelm us. If we reverse our focus and look at ourselves the way God views us, we realize that the obstacles and problems are not as huge as we think; in fact, we will be able to overcome them all.

In the past, I have looked at my obstacles and seen them in relation to my limitations; and from my perspective, overcoming them seemed virtually impossible. The ovarian cyst was a demonstration of this. I did not consider that when God saw my obstacles, He looked at it in relation to His infinite wisdom. Being without limitations means that with God, all things are possible. Our obstacles become but a speck to Him. As you know, I did become pregnant and had children; and after the first pregnancy, the cyst depleted. My problem was nothing in God's eyes.

When we look at our problems, what should we do? We should practice looking at our lives and everything that comes with life as God sees them: as a speck in God's universe.

Properly Set Your Perspective

In your travels, you will face many mountains, valleys, and hills. None of these can compare to God. He is greater, stronger, and more magnificent than anything you can face. If your perspective of God is not one that properly sees Him as described in the Bible, it must change. Your journey requires the correct perspective. Make the choice now to believe Him as He is. A change in your perspective of God will definitely change how you see your obstacles.

Self-Reflection Activity

Complete the following activity and be sure to journal your thoughts.

- Read the following scriptures and consider what they mean to you: Numbers 13:27–33.
- Do you really see God as being Sovereign, above all, and greater than any giant?
- How do you react when an obstacle comes? Do you believe what God has already said in His Word, no matter how big the problem?

Next Steps

Psalms 95:3–4 reads, "For the LORD is the great God, the great King above all gods. In his hand are the depths of the earth..." According to this scripture, there is none greater than God. Begin to put Him in His proper place in your heart. This even means above what you see, because we do not walk by what we see but by our faith in God. As you do this, you will see that your problems are minimized by God's greatness.

MATURITY AND THE BLESSING OF TRIALS

Hearing by the Word of God...

"Consider it pure joy, my brothers, whenever you face trials of many kinds, because you know that the testing of your faith develops perseverance. Perseverance must finish its work so that you may be mature and complete, not lacking anything..." (James 1:2–4).

"Why do you quietly sit back and say nothing when you have so much to say? You are a minister of the Gospel. Open your mouth and speak!"

This is something my spiritual father emphatically said to me. His speech caught me off guard because I had never imagined hearing those words from him and with such seriousness and passion. I had asked God to show me my purpose in life, but this was not what I expected. I did not accept his words immediately. I did not want to be considered a minister in any sense of the word. It took a few years to pass and a couple of relocations before I considered them; but as Mary did, I hid them in my heart.

In the course of time, God revealed even more to me regarding my purpose. I was to deliver His message of restoration to women. The more revelation I received, the more excited I became. I realized these things were rooted heavily in my heart. I now understood my service to the Body of Christ to a greater degree. It was not long before women began sharing their life experiences with me. I would offer God's truth to them as they came to me, and also words of encouragement to get them through their situations.

There is no feeling like knowing you have a purpose and are actually fulfilling it. Unfortunately, I believed that what I did was not well-received by everyone. Things quickly became very uncomfortable for me, especially after I presented my personal ministry plans to church leadership. Initially, I was given the "okay" to move forward. However, when these plans were put into action, things were not okay.

My ministry was one that operated outside of the church, so I was challenged in my commitment to the church, especially with regards to my role as a female leader. I endured what I perceived as negative comments, simply because I tried to encourage sisters in Christ. I did not understand this, and I questioned, "Lord, why is this happening when I am doing what You have given me to do? This is not supposed to happen in the church." The level of opposition that I experienced caused me to question many things, even my purpose. I even put some things on hold. I had to seek God. I soon found that this experience was another sure proof that blessings can come from trials. You might ask, "How so?" I will explain.

A Contradiction of Terms?

I realize that using the word "blessing" in combination with the word "trial" might seem like a contradiction of terms. One might ask, "How can there be a blessing in going through something painful? Surely the times when we are struggling and can barely keep our heads above water cannot be considered a blessing." I can honestly say that there are times when we are truly blessed in our struggles; we see it every day.

An Example from Childbirth

The human reproductive process is a wonderful miracle and a good example of being blessed in struggle. As we know, after a woman becomes pregnant, she carries the baby for approximately nine months. During those months, a great deal is taking place in both the bodies of the mother and child. The closer a woman gets to delivery, the more uncomfortable things become. For some, the discomfort starts early. There are the back pains, bones separating, Charlie horses in the middle of the night, and often morning sickness. There is the poking and prodding of the doctor; and once delivery time comes, there is the extreme discomfort of labor pains.

During the pregnancy of my second son, my doctor joked that every time he saw me, I looked increasingly ready to give birth. That was because carrying another person inside of me was not easy; it was downright challenging. There were days when I just did not want to get out of bed and everything seemed to be a great effort. Yet, in spite of all of this, women all over the world willingly bear the process. We know that our condition is temporary, and soon we will hold our little blessing in our arms. We have hope because we know at the end, a beautiful child comes forth. Even after enduring this process once, some do it again. Why? Like Jesus said:

> *"A woman giving birth to a child has pain because her time has come; but when her baby is born she forgets the anguish because of her joy that a child is born into the world"(John 16:21).*

If we want to bring children into the world, we cannot skip the process of pregnancy and childbirth. During the process, there is a waiting period where growth and maturity takes place. Sure, there are some frustrations and pain; but God is skillfully forming this being within our womb that is unlike any other. Yes, the process is painful and exhausting; but it is needed for the child to come forth.

Accepting Trials with Joy

We also find ourselves having to endure many other painful processes, and naturally we want the struggle to be over as soon as possible because we are hurting. However, we also have the capability to know that the trial is temporary, just like pregnancy. If we can endure the struggle, we will come to find that the transformation taking place is a beautiful one, and we realize that without the process, the growth will not occur.

When I first read that we should count our trials as joy, I could not fathom why we would do this. But the more I look back at the trials that God has led me through, the more I see the great blessing and discipline that came forth as a result. In my earlier example, my faith in my God-given purpose had been tested. But I learned to persevere in this area. It also challenged me to love those who I felt were doing me wrong. I wish I can say that I did all of the right things and remained in a constant state of joy, but I did not. I did, however, recognize the growth that resulted from this experience.

I would like to rejoice in all things and I am learning small steps at a time. How about you? Do you think you can rejoice in the midst of your trial? I believe with God's help, we all can. The Bible says that after the apostles had been called before the Sanhedrin and flogged, they rejoiced in the fact that they were found worthy to suffer disgrace for the sake of Christ (Acts 5:41). They welcomed trials and struggles; they understood that they were a part of their growth. They saw the trials as opportunities. Because as we endure the tribulations, our faith is tested; and as our faith is tested, patience is developed within us. As patience is developed, we are fashioned into maturity and completeness in Christ.

What About Your Trials?

This book focuses on equipping you for challenges you may face while on your road to victory. You can be sure that you will be met with trials. Instead of dreading them, change how you view them. A change in thinking on how you endure trials can make a vast difference in the journey. As you continue on this road, consider that each trial you face is an avenue of maturity. Remember that the ultimate result of your trial is a more-perfect you. A former trial is likely preparing you for the next section of road ahead. What do you think? Can you see your trials as blessings?

Self-Reflection Activity

Complete the following activity and be sure to journal your thoughts.

- Read the following scriptures and consider what they mean to you: James 1:2–4; James 1:12.
- Looking back on previous trials, can you see where growth took place as a result?
- Is your attitude to patiently endure a trial? If not, how have you handled your trials, and in what ways can you improve your response to trials?

Next Steps

James 1:2–4 reads, "Consider it pure joy, my brothers, whenever you face trials of many kinds, because you know that the testing of your faith develops perseverance. Perseverance must finish its work so that you may be mature and complete, not lacking anything." Resolve to deal with all challenges by applying this scripture. Picture the end result, which is maturity, instead of focusing on the trial itself. If you fail at taking on this attitude in the beginning, do not give up! Keep pushing!

APPRECIATE THE RAIN

Hearing by the Word of God...

"Land that drinks in the rain often falling on it and that produces a crop useful to those for whom it is farmed receives the blessing of God" (Hebrews 6:7).

There was an occasion when my mentor challenged me so severely, I became very angry with her. I had travelled back to my hometown of Detroit and hosted an event at the church that she and her husband pastor. Because the ladies that normally worked with me could not travel, we made arrangements for others to help out. Putting together the event was quite difficult because we were not face-to-face. To accommodate, we had phone meetings and email instructions about the details. Unfortunately, on the day of the event, things did not go as I had planned. I was not happy about the outcome, but I did not say anything. However, I am one of those people with very-animated facial expressions.

My mentor noticed my displeasure and we talked about it. During our conversation, she challenged my thought process. I normally welcomed her critiques because most times she was right, and her desire was for me to grow. However, on this occasion, I felt she was not looking at the entire picture. She told me that I needed to learn leadership skills. She did not back down, either, no matter how much I argued my case. When I left to fly back home, I was still very angry about it. After a week or two, I called and apologized. I realized the people had volunteered their time and efforts, and they deserved gratitude for their service, no matter how things turned out. She accepted my apology, but reiterated her previous points: that I needed to take leadership training. She challenged me to move beyond my comfort zone, of which I finally accepted.

Difficulty Compared to a Storm

Many times, the challenges and difficulties of life are compared to a storm. The reason for this is because a storm is loud, difficult, and sometimes scary. Life's challenges seem to take on these same characteristics. Sometimes you cannot see what is ahead of you when the rain is coming down, and this situation can be very unnerving. Most of us would avoid storms if we could. I am not sure about you, but I do not wake up and say, "I hope a good storm blows in today." Why? Because things are easier when the skies are sunny. We do not know what to expect from the storm. We cannot determine how long we will have to endure it. We cannot foresee how it will impact us. These unknowns are uncomfortable.

Rain Alters Our Plans

As a child, I did not really care for any kind of rain, whether it was a light drizzle or a heavy storm. Rain usually meant that we could not go outside, play, or do what we wanted. I remember hearing adults say rainy weather was perfect for sleeping, and I did not understand why this would be. The Bible teaches us that as long as the earth remains, there will be seedtime and harvest time (Genesis 8:22). Without rain, there is no harvest. The funny thing is, as an adult, I did not appreciate rain until I bought my house. I saw how costly the water bill was from watering my lawn on a frequent basis. After paying expensive water bills, I began thanking God every time it rained. As I grew and matured, I quickly realized that the rain was actually to our benefit as human beings. This is the same for us spiritually. As we grow, we can learn to appreciate the spiritual rain because it produces growth in our spiritual walk with God.

The Benefits

As spiritual children, we may not like the storms of life because we do not realize how they are working on our behalf. As we mature in Christ, we come to embrace the rain because we see how it helps us. We realize that without spiritual rain, there is no growth in our souls. Furthermore, just as the rain in nature can change from a light drizzle to a heavy downpour, the same can be for our spiritual life.

Many people do not like natural rain because it is messy; and if it is a downpour, it makes maneuvering within our lives harder. But as adults, when we are indoors and protected, we can learn to appreciate the sound of the rain as well as its usefulness. Many even come to find the sound of the rain to be soothing. The same can occur for us spiritually because we are inside God's protection. We can appreciate the atmosphere of life's struggles because we know we are protected. During spiritual storms, we find ourselves drawing closer to God because we are crying out to Him and depending on Him more. Afterward, we see how our relationship with Him has grown, and we are better equipped to deal with problems in the future. As this process continues, we come to take these situations as opportunities of growth, to draw closer and to know God better.

A Useful Outcome

The scripture below is a depiction of what happens when the rain is absorbed by the land; it processes something useful for the farmer.

> *"Land that drinks in the rain often falling on it and that produces a crop useful to those for whom it is farmed receives the blessing of God"* *(Hebrews 6:7).*

At the end of the trial, something is produced. As we appreciate the trials, we can allow them to produce something within us that is useful to God.

In my earlier example, I did finally accept what my mentor said, and began taking the leadership classes that my job offered. I found these to be very helpful, both on and off the job. My manager also knew that I was taking these classes. What I did not realize is the following year I would be promoted for the second time in two years! The entire situation that started off as an unwanted challenge led to a promotion. Who would have thought?

I want to encourage you that your trial can produce something useful in you. Yes, they are difficult and painful; but there is an end. As a believer, you can be assured that no matter how scary the storm may be, it cannot hurt you. It cannot alter your path to victory. When the enemy comes upon you, like a flood, God raises the standard around you (Isaiah 59:19). In God, you are protected from the spiritual floods. As you continue to grow and mature on this journey, you can become so confident in God's protection that you appreciate the rain.

Self-Reflection Activity

Complete the following activity and be sure to journal your thoughts.

- Read the following scriptures and consider what they mean to you: Genesis 8:22; Isaiah 43:2; James 1:2–3.
- Can you see yourself embracing life's storms, knowing that they will produce growth?
- What can you do during a storm to keep your focus on the protection of God?

Next Steps

Hebrews 6:7 reads, "Land that drinks in the rain often falling on it and that produces a crop useful to those for whom it is farmed receives the blessing of God." This Lesson is so closely related to the previous one, but the distinct difference is that we focus on welcoming the rain as we realize the need for it. Here, I will ask that instead of running from the storms of life, use them so that they water the seed of God's Word; allow them to produce a crop that God can use for His Kingdom.

LOOK BEYOND
THE CLOUDS

Hearing by the Word of God...

*"By faith Abraham, even though he was past age–and Sarah herself
was barren–was enabled to become a father because he considered
him faithful who had made the promise.*

*And so from this one man, and he as good as dead, came
descendants as numerous as the stars in the sky and as countless as
the sand on the seashore" (Hebrews 11:11-12).*

It was the last Sunday that I would attend my church in Detroit. The time had come for me to relocate to New York City
with my husband. We were both in attendance. He had come
to spend Christmas with my family and drive me to New York.
My pastor announced that I was moving away. Many people
congratulated us. For the first time in this situation, I was
afraid. In that moment, I realized that I would not know anyone else in my new home state. Then, after the announcement,
the worship leader looked at me and began to sing, "For I know
the plans I have for you..." I did not know then how much that
song would mean to me. Those words, which are also a Bible

verse, would be a promise that would help me through our first years of marriage. Both the song and the scripture speak of God's good plan for the Israelites after their time of suffering (Jeremiah 29:11).

As things would turn out, the first years of marriage were rough. Among other things, my husband and I were both in our thirties and independent. We both had ideas about everything, but they did not always line up. Sometimes making a decision was like a game of tug of war. I must admit: I was headstrong. Since I had no family or friends there with me, when we argued, I had nowhere to go. I also had a hard time adjusting to the city; it was overwhelming for me. The subways, the crowds, the rooster that crowed at 5 am. Yes, I said rooster. For some reason the building "super" had a rooster on the side of the apartment building. We fast forwarded our plans to relocate to a warmer climate, and landed jobs in Dallas, Texas. This time, we both had no family or friends, just the two of us.

Even in this foreign territory, we still played tug of war. I remember one night when we had another bad argument. Things did not look good. I sat, crying in the bathroom. I had waited so long to meet someone to marry. Once I committed my life to Christ, I had intentionally waited for a man that knew God. These types of arguments were not supposed to happen because we were both believers. We eventually called my spiritual father and his wife back in Detroit. They encouraged and counseled us through this time, using great wisdom and the Word of God. I am still very much thankful to them.

The Promise Remains

One day, my family and I were riding along the freeway, heading to our weekly ritual of daycare and work. This particular morning, the sky looked overcast; the weather report indicated a strong chance of rain. As my husband drove and my toddler son sat in the back seat, I gazed out of the window into the sky. The picture was amazing. I noticed that there were multiple levels of clouds in the sky. The clouds closest to the earth were dark and gloomy, but the ones lifted higher into the sky were puffy and white, surrounded by the beautiful blue sky. I sat in awe at the sight, and noticed for the first time beauty in the midst of gloom. It is amazing how God allows us to see things we have never noticed before.

Believe the Promise Giver

The Bible tells us in Hebrews 12 that we have witnesses of Christ who have gone before us. The significant group of people are mentioned in Hebrews 11. They demonstrated their faith while enduring hardship, which testified of the impending coming of our Messiah. This record gives us an idea of the horrendous things that some of these people endured. They most certainly had lives filled with rain clouds, but they *believed the One Who promised.*

The Example of Abraham

Let's look at one strong man of faith. Abraham received the promise of an offspring in his old age as well as the promise of becoming a father to many nations. It took about twenty-five years for Abraham and Sarah to receive Isaac, the fulfillment of God's promise. Years after Isaac was born, God tested Abraham by instructing him to present Isaac as a sacrifice. He set out to obey God in offering up the very son who was promised to him. He looked beyond that trial and only saw the promise that God had made. Abraham was only able to endure this task because he knew that he would become the father to many; and he knew that would only happen through Isaac. He did not know how it would happen, and he did not have to know; he simply believed in the Promise Giver. So, he looked beyond that cloud that was directly before him and saw that blue sky that was afar off.

My Blue Sky

I believe God used the worship leader that day we sat in my church in Detroit. It was God's promise to me. Sometimes when times became rough, I thought of that day. It was the promise that still remained despite the clouds. It has now been ten years, and God has done amazing things in both of us. We are not playing tug of war anymore, well maybe on occasion. But you know what? That promise still remains. I understand now that what we went through was not rare. The first few years of marriage take some adjustment, and will likely be the opposite of a fairy tale. But the words to that song helped me. In essence, God was preparing me for what was ahead.

I know the plans I have for you
I know just what you're going through
So when you can't see
What tomorrow holds
And yesterday is through,
Remember I know,
The plans I have for you

To give you hope for tomorrow
Joy for your sorrow
Strength for everything you go through
Remember I know the plans I have for you

"I KNOW THE PLANS"
Words and Music by Martha D. Munizzi (BMI)
© 2003 Say The Name Publishing
All rights reserved. Used by permission

A Word of Caution

Just like the many witnesses that have gone ahead of us, we can faithfully endure until the end. But to do this, we have to be willing to throw off the things that hinder us. Remember that our hindrances are not only trials; the Bible also tells us that the sin in our lives hinders us as well (Hebrews 12:1). We cannot allow sin to be the thing that keeps us from moving forward. Continuing our journeys depends on it. Instead, we must throw it as far away as we can. Then we can look to Jesus who has both authored and finished our race.

Look to Your Savior

Your hope in the coming salvation has to be anchored. You must determine that rain or sin cannot stop you. How can you do this? By reflecting on our Savior, the One who endured the cross. He disregarded the shame just for you. He knew about your journey long before you did. He promised you victory in the end. To endure, you can do what He did: You can look beyond the rain clouds to the promise. Think of this so that you do not give up during the cloudy days. In the end, you will find yourself in the midst of the promise.

Self-Reflection Activity

Complete the following activity and be sure to journal your thoughts.

- Read the following scriptures and consider what they mean to you: Hebrews 4:14; Hebrews 12:1–3.
- When the clouds of life come along, have you been able to look beyond them to see the blue sky (the promises)?
-

Next Steps

Hebrews 11:11–12 reads, "By faith Abraham, even though he was past age–and Sarah herself was barren–was enabled to become a father because he considered him faithful who had made the promise. And so from this one man, and he as good as dead, came descendants as numerous as the stars in the sky and as countless as the sand on the seashore." What keeps us going in this world is the promise of our Lord. This assignment requires that you build your faith in God. Take a stand to believe God, in spite of the clouds right before you; and push forward to see His promises. Go through your Bible and write down some of the promises you see. (For example: *Hebrews 13:5 "... 'Never will I leave you; never will I forsake you.'"*)

BECOME A BEARER OF GODLY FRUIT

Hearing by the Word of God...

"Blessed is the man who does not walk in the counsel of the wicked or stand in the way of sinners or sit in the seat of mockers. But his delight is in the law of the Lord, and on His law he meditates day and night. He is like a tree planted by streams of water, which yields its fruit in season and whose leaf does not wither. Whatever he does prospers"
(Psalms 1:1-3).

When I proclaimed my commitment to Christ, I went on a quest of learning. If we are encouraged to "hunger and thirst" after righteousness, I was devouring the Bible. I had tried to read it in the past and failed. One day, a friend of mine gave me a translation that was much easier to read and I became intrigued. I was learning about God, who He is and what He thinks of us. My eyes were opened to Truth.

It is true that the Word of God is living and active and sharper than a double-edged sword. It cuts deeply in some cases. When reading it and applying it to my life, things were much clearer. I learned what to do in certain situations. I learned of my responsibility to obey the Word. I realized in areas where I neglected the Word, I had opened myself to certain hardships. The more I read it, the more my faith increased. Jesus said, *"They that hunger and thirst for righteousness shall be filled."* I did not recognize that His Word was filling me until I realized it caused me to have "an apt reply in season." I mentioned before that women would share their situations with me. At first I wondered why they came to me with their deepest concerns. I never intentionally gave off anything that said, "Hey come over here to me. I have answers for you." I did not know what to say or do, but soon realized that the right scripture would come to mind. Sometimes a lesson I had recently learned in my personal study time would be what that person needed to hear. I was amazed. The Word of God produced within me fruit useful for those around me. I was bearing fruit.

The Tree Analogy

When my husband and I had our home built, we noticed that the builder planted two trees in front of every house in our subdivision. In their initial state, these trees were thin and fragile. Apparently, special care and attention was needed to ensure these trees' maturity and stability. If care was not taken, they faced the possibility of dying and never producing fruit, theoretically never serving their purpose. In fact, one of our trees died a slow death and never grew to be of any benefit to its environment. Over the next couple of years that followed, we began to see the affects of bad weather on these trees; some leaned and some had to be removed because they were damaged.

Special Care Needed

In several places in the Bible, man is compared to a tree. In the very first Psalm, we are told that the one who focuses on the Word of God is blessed; he is like a tree that is planted next to water, always bearing fruit when it is time. A tree planted next to a stream of water never lacks sustenance because its nourishing source is always by its side. Because of this, the tree is healthy and good for fruit. So it is with mankind; if special care and attention is taken to walk with God and to learn from Him, we become rooted and grounded in Him. We become people who produce a lifestyle that enhances others and brings glory to our Maker. God is our Source of spiritual nourishment. Apart from God, our nourishment comes from the world and its influence; so whatever we produce could be damaging to those around us.

A Vine and Its Branches

Jesus used a slightly different twist on the tree analogy. He told us that He was the Vine and we are the branches. As long as we remain in Him, we can bear much fruit. Apart from Him, we are powerless to do anything. Through this, we see that our focus and reliance on God is of great importance. How do we abide in Him? We do this by reading, studying, and meditating His Word. As we find ourselves absorbed in Him, we become rooted. Like the tree, our roots run deep; we are stable. We can sustain the torrential rains that confront us in life. As we previously learned, the rains have to come. However, James tells us what to do with these rains. He tells us to appreciate them and be joyous when they come; because in the face of trial, our faith is tested. While this testing occurs, perseverance starts to do its work, and we are matured. In order for us to mature, our faith requires testing, and in order for our faith to be tested, we must face trials.

We Must Mature

Like the tree, we can use the trials to our advantage. We can allow them to produce good fruit in our lives. Jesus told us that a tree can be identified by the fruit that it produces. Jesus teaches us how to discern others by the things they do. In the same vein, others can also know who we belong to by our fruit. Thus, we find that we also have to evaluate ourselves to ensure that we are a benefit to His Kingdom. We must ensure that we do not remain like those frail trees that were initially planted. When we first come to Christ, we are very fragile; we have no footing because our roots are shallow. But there has to come a time in our Christian walk when all that we have learned takes effect, and we become good trees with fruit that can benefit others. There has to come a time when we are no longer just receiving but also giving of our fruit.

It's Time to Bear Fruit

Part of your journey to victory involves maturing. During your travels, you will meet others along the way. As you mature, you will have fruit to give. I want you to consider that your journey is not just about you but about others as well. Be sure to abide in Jesus by abiding in the Word so that you can bear His fruit. The fruit you bear can bless the life of another.

Self-Reflection Activity

Complete the following activity and be sure to journal your thoughts.

- Read the following scriptures and consider what they mean to you: Psalms 1:1–3; John 15:1–5; Matthew 7:15–20.
- Have you reached a place in Christianity where it is obvious that Christ is in you by the things you do?
- Are you able to affect those around you with God's Kingdom because you are now bearing His fruit?

Next Steps

John 15:4–5 reads, "Remain in me, and I will remain in you. No branch can bear fruit by itself; it must remain in the vine. Neither can you bear fruit unless you remain in me. I am the vine; you are the branches. If a man remains in me and I in him, he will bear much fruit; apart from me you can do nothing." When Jesus lived on earth, He was the Word of God in flesh form. The way that we remain in Jesus is by abiding in His Word and allowing His Word to abide in us. Earlier, I asked that you start setting aside quiet time with the Lord on a daily basis. If you have not already, begin to incorporate time to study the Bible and apply its instructions to your life. Allow it to transform you so that you find yourself bearing the Spirit's fruit (love, joy, peace, patience, kindness, goodness, faithfulness, gentleness, and self-control).

LIFE WOULD BE LOST WITHOUT CHRIST

Hearing by the Word of God...

"Behold, I stand at the door, and knock: if any man hear My Voice, and open the door, I will come in to him, and will sup with him, and he with me" (Revelation 3:20 KJV).

My aunt wanted the best for me; she would challenge me in my academics. She was an intelligent woman in her own rights, but she chose a different path. She pushed me to learn and to earn better grades. She wanted for me what she did not attain.

I mentioned earlier that my maternal grandmother died at an early age. I failed to mention that she led a carefree lifestyle and was dependent on alcohol. My aunt mourned her mother's death for the rest of her life, but eventually took to the same path. My uncles joined her down this road, but they all wanted better for me. My aunt was the most verbal in relaying this message. She scolded me when I received a "C" on my report cards. My mother explained that this was her way of making sure I did my best; and it worked. I went on to attend college and obtained a Bachelor's of Science, the first in my family to do so. I know she was proud. Societally, I had become successful, but it did not stop me from making my own bad choices.

Needless to say, I was not dating Christians at the time. One day, I found myself in situation that shook me. I had visited someone, and while there, they had some surprise visitors. I was told to stay in the room until I got the okay to come out. I was terrified. I did not know what they were doing or why I could not come out. I could not make a peep. I remembered thinking, "Who is this? What have I gotten myself into? I did not spend five and a half years in college to be in this situation. What if they found me here and became upset?" This experience was enough for me, and I determined that something had to change. Around this time, a friend encouraged me to seek God, so I did. I resisted Him for many years, but no longer.

After finding my Savior, I was compelled to write a poem on how my life would have been like if I had kept resisting Him. It is a reflection on what life was like prior to coming into relationship with Him, and a look forward into the hope I had because of Him.

It is essential that we never lose sight of what Christ has done for us in our salvation, so I pray this poem blesses you.

What If

What if God had given up on me
When He knocked and I did not open?
What if He had given up on me?
I would still be walking the path of life in total darkness,
Stubbing my toe against the trees of this world
That have roots of evil.
I would still be guessing at which course to take
At the fork in the road.

What if He had given up on me?
I would be lacking the
"Peace that surpasses understanding!"
I would be lacking the "joy unspeakable!"
I would be lacking "the standard" that He "raises"
To protect me when my "enemy
Comes upon me like a flood!"
What if He had given up on me?
My hope would be continuously deferred,
Leaving me feeling hopeless when the trials come
In this roller coaster called life.

Thank God He did not give up on me!
When He continued to knock at my door,
When I finally opened and said "come in."
Thank God He did not give up on me because…
Now He has become unto me
"A lamp to my feet and a light to my path"
To guide me on the journey of life!

Thank God He did not give up on me!
For I would not have known
The truth so that it could set me free.
Thank God He did not give up on me
The last time He said,
"Behold, I stand at the door, and knock: if any man hear
My Voice, and open the door, I will come in to him, and
Will sup with him, and he with me."

Self-Reflection Activity

Complete the following activity and be sure to journal your thoughts.

- Read the following scriptures and consider what they mean to you: Revelation 3:20.
- What would your life be like if Christ had not died for you?

Next Steps

Psalm 95:1–2 reads, "Come, let us sing for joy to the LORD; let us shout aloud to the Rock of our salvation. Let us come before him with thanksgiving and extol him with music and song." Our God loves for His people to acknowledge and appreciate Him; so today, spend some time in praise unto God. Thank Him for His mercies and grace towards you. Celebrate His love by letting Him know that you are grateful to Him.

DO NOT HARDEN YOUR HEART

Hearing by the Word of God...

"Harden not your hearts, as in the provocation, in the day of temptation in the wilderness" (Hebrews 3:8 KJV).

I am the eldest of all my siblings. In fact, I am almost a decade older than the sister next in line. Because of this, I am a nurturer by nature. This began with my birth family and later included friends. My family and friends relied on me to help them if what they needed was within reason. And when I joined my church, I immediately began serving.

At the time, I was single and had no children; so I had a large amount of time on my hands. I was a member of the women's dance ministry and loved it. I also began teaching the little girl's dance team. Between my family, friends, and church, I soon found myself very busy. Before I knew it, I served those around me in a capacity that left me feeling overwhelmed. I was doing too much, giving of both my time and resources. Being overly busy caused me to grow weary. The attitudes of those around me caused me to feel unappreciated, which also left me feeling disappointed. I guess since I was a nurturer, I was expected to "be there" for everyone. However, the toxic combination of weariness, feeling unappreciated, and disappointment led to a change in my attitude. This attitude eventually impacted my heart and it became hardened.

A Heart Issue

> *"'Even now,' declares the Lord, 'return to me with all your heart, with fasting and weeping and mourning. Rend your heart and not your garments. Return to the LORD your God, for he is gracious and compassionate, slow to anger and abounding in love'" (Joel 2:12-13).*

I have read this scripture before, but one day, a greater meaning leapt off the page. In the days of the Old Testament, to show grief, the Jews would rend, or tear, their clothes. This was an outward expression of what was supposed to be felt within their hearts. In this day, many have been hardened by life's challenges. With a hardened heart, a person cannot genuinely "rend" their heart toward God.

Uncontrollable Circumstances: What to Do?

One of the associate pastors at my previous church said there would be circumstances beyond our control; but what we would do about them? I later thought about his question. There will be disappointments. We will be taken for granted. There will be people who treat us wrongly. There will be mishaps; but what will we do about them? Do we think we can avoid these matters or do we give up?

The Danger of Building Walls

Often times, we make big mistakes in handling matters by simply refusing to listen to the Word of God. In trying to handle situations on our own, we tend to go into avoidance mode. We clam up and harden our hearts, or we erect a wall so circumstances will not affect us. The problem with this is when we harden ourselves in this way, we are doing so in every way, even toward God. This form of protection (human protection) takes away your ability to love and to live freely. If you do not believe me, look at some of the people around us who we may say are hardened and unresponsive. Do they look happy? Do they have good things to say? Do they freely express themselves? The Bible says,

> *"In the same way you judge others, you will be judged, and with the measure you use, it will be measured to you"(Matthew 7:2).*

Most of us know people who show no emotion, have no trust, who do and say things that seem wrong or hurtful; and we simply think they are mean or horrible people. Many times, I have judged people in my heart and have asked, "Why are they such jerks?" I did not realize what I was doing, and I soon found out why they were "jerks." I discovered that in some situations, people are like this as a result of "protecting themselves" or hardening their hearts. Through personal experiences, I once received a very clear message on this.

I Built a Wall of Protection

I mentioned how I felt overwhelmed, unappreciated, and disappointed. Circumstances left me feeling like I was giving too much time and effort toward the needs of others at the expense of myself. I pretty much dropped everything and decided I was not doing anything else. In short, I chose to harden my heart. I still loved God, but things slowly started changing. There was no passion for Him. When I read the Bible, it was just words on paper; and while I knew something was wrong, I could not put my finger on it. I knew He was there, and He continued to answer my prayers. However, our relationship was not the same, and I knew it had to do with me.

"Harden not your hearts, as in the provocation, in the day of tempta-
tion in the wilderness." (Hebrews 3:8 KJV).

If you noticed, this scripture basically says not to harden your heart when provoked in the wilderness. This scripture was a warning to us New-Testament believers. It is a lesson from the children of Israel's mistakes. God tested them in the desert to know what was in their hearts and to see whether they would obey His commands (Deuteronomy 8:2). The pressures of their testing provoked them, and their response was a hardened heart toward God. As you know, our journeys are filled with trials and testing. These can provoke us; but we are not to allow our hearts to become stiff, for if we do, it will impact our devotion towards God.

The Wall Keeps God Out

The Bible says that "God is love" (1 John 4:16). How can love dwell in a hardened heart? In my case, I missed our relationship; but I could not get back to it, no matter what I did. Due to this blockage, I literally could not cry out to Him. I could not rend my heart. Everyone who knows me knows that I am a sensitive person, a trait for which I am now grateful; but my friends and loved ones quickly noticed that something was wrong. Everything I did was external; I "tore" my clothes, so to speak, but not my heart. It took some time for me to even see what God was showing me about myself. I now understand those people I spoke of earlier, and can pray for their peace instead of resenting them. I can pray that God would show them what He showed me because my heart was now torn; it bleeds for Him once more.

God's Peace Protects Our Hearts

The message here is that in life, difficulties will occur often; but if we give our hearts to God, He will protect us.

"And the peace of God, which transcends all understanding, will guard your hearts and your minds in Christ Jesus" (Philippians 4:7).

I have come to this conclusion: I would rather live a life being hurt and allowing God's healing to take place than to be hardened and not have the ability to love.

I am sure that your life has not been absent of heartache in some way. If you have hardened your heart, give it back to God to make whole. *"The Lord is near to the brokenhearted and saves those who are crushed in spirit" (Psalms 34:18 NASB).* On your journey, there will be provocation; however, resist the urge to build walls. Instead, allow God's peace to guard your heart. You can trust Him with it. He will protect it for the entire journey.

Self-Reflection Activity

Complete the following activity and be sure to journal your thoughts.

- Read the following scriptures and consider what they mean to you: Joel 2:13; Philippians 4:7.
- Have you allowed life circumstances to harden your heart?
- How do you see the hardness of your heart a ecting your relationship with God and how you treat others?
- Do you practice allowing God to guard your heart rather than keeping your own wall of protection around it?

Next Steps

Proverbs 4:20–23 reads, "My son, pay attention to what I say; listen closely to my words. Do not let them out of your sight, keep them within your heart; for they are life to those who find them and health to a man's whole body. Above all else, guard your heart, for it is the wellspring of life." The state of our heart is important because it determines our attitude towards God and others. There is no way to keep the two greatest commands, to love God and love our neighbor, if our hearts are cold. Today, search your heart and determine if you are holding an unforgiving grudge against someone. Rid yourself of resentment by releasing those who have o ended you. This is so crucial because you cannot fully give your heart to Christ if there are people that you have not forgiven.

WORSHIP COMES FROM THE HEART

Hearing by the Word of God...

"'These people come near to me with their mouth and honor me with their lips, but their hearts are far from me. Their worship of me is made up only of rules taught by men'" (Isaiah 29:13).

I enjoy expressions of worship and praise. They are an overflow of my heart's contents. I have learned that the road to victory requires a love and gratitude toward God. Through ups and downs, we see God working in our favor; and the result should be a thankful heart. I especially like dance, singing, and the worship of God through instruments. The first time I saw a team worship in dance, I felt love in my heart. This was different from watching a dance performance. The dancers were overwhelmed with praise and adoration for the Lord. By end of the song, the congregation had fully joined in worship. It was awesome! I wanted to do that. I wanted to outwardly express what I felt inside to God. So, I joined the team, and it was a wonderful experience. We meditated on the words of the songs, studied supporting scriptures, and the dances were choreographed in a way to express the song's meaning. It was definitely a ministry. I would like to think for all of us, the outward expression was a result of what resided inwardly.

Expressions of the Heart

Jesus said that loving God is the greatest commandment. I believe our love for Him is the glue that holds our entire walk together. Love prompts action. Love causes a desire to please the one we love. It stimulates us to sing songs to God.

When we lift our hands in the midst of a worship service, what does it means? When we dance or jump or cry or fall to our knees or shout for joy, what does it mean? When some of us stand in stillness with pure awe in our hearts, and nothing but tears of joy can fall from our eyes, what does it mean? We do these things because of our love and adoration for God. We think of who He is and what He has brought into our lives. We think of how He has forgiven us. We praise Him for what He has done. We celebrate Him with great joy for our victories. Our hearts leap in the midst of our praise, realizing His wonder. As Jeremiah said, "like fire shut up in my bones." The closer we grow in relationship to our God, our love grows even deeper. Our praise means so much more, and we are less able to contain it. We give way to the expression of our love.

Settled in Routine

Sadly, for some, this magnitude of praise towards God fizzles away. This has happened to me. At times, I have become so busy that I did not remember the great things that He has done in my life. Even circumstances have captured my focus instead of the One who deserves it. Such occurrences can cause our relationship to detach. This distance from God causes me to no longer praise or worship Him as He deserves. I cannot give my adoration to the One who has covered me under the shadow of His wings. I hate to say it, but sometimes when I have entered the sanctuary and lifted my hands and voice in songs, I am only going through motions. Occasionally, I am simply responding to the direction of the worship leader, and my mind is not on God; my heart is not into the worship.

Unjoyful Noise to the Lord

When I am in mindless, heartless praise, is that really praise? If I am screaming and shouting, and my heart is not in it, am I just a "sounding gong" making noise? If in an effort to stir up praise in the congregation, the preacher says, "If you love the Lord, I dare you to say, 'Hallelujah!'", is my reaction because I do not want to be the oddball refusing to participate, or is my reaction unto God? By offering empty praise, have I actually displeased the One who is really important to me? The Lord says:

> *"These people come near to me with their mouth and honor me with their lips, but their hearts are far from me. Their worship of me is made up only of rules taught by men"(Isaiah 29:13).*

In Joel, we are admonished to *"rend [our] heart and not [our] garment" (Joel 2:13)*. We must praise God from our heart, with sincerity and not just for the outward appearance. There is no gain in doing our "acts of righteousness before men, to be seen by them," because if we do, we "will have no reward from your Father in heaven" (Matthew 6:1).

A Return to Genuine Praise

My spiritual father, Pastor Willie Myles of Detroit, Michigan, once said to me that most people do not praise God because they do not have the revelation of who He is; and they have not seen what He has done in their lives. Sadly, even those of us who have gotten this revelation still allow our zeal for God to fall by the wayside. How do we return to a genuine praise unto God? We can look at the patriarchs in the Bible and learn from the sincerity in their praise.

The book of Psalms is full of those who understood that God was the One responsible for giving them strength, saving them from their enemies, or providing for their needs. They were so compelled by God's faithfulness that they wrote and sang songs about it. They knew that their lives were held in the palms of their Maker's hands. They knew every aspect of their lives involved Him. They realized their victories were because of Him.

Likewise, as we open our eyes to see God's work, our hearts once again rend before Him. We become fully appreciative, and our worship and praises are again a beautiful sound. This is our offering of sacrifice unto Him. Done from the heart, it is a "sweet savor" going up before God, a pleasing aroma. His nature and faithfulness to us warrants sincere displays of adoration.

He Deserves Your Love

In every obstacle we face, our God has been our ever-present help. He guides us over many bumps and hurdles. He saves some of us from "the bear and the lion." He has opened doors that no one can shut. I can say so many things about His work in our lives. My point is, our journeys will not be possible without Him. I want to encourage you to give to Him the recognition He deserves. Give to Him your undying love. Let Him know that you are glad He is there. Finally, be sure to maintain a committed heart toward God through heartfelt worship unto Him.

Self-Reflection Activity

Complete the following activity and be sure to journal your thoughts.

- Read the following scriptures and consider what they mean to you: Joel 2:13; Isaiah 29:13.
- Do you sometimes find yourself going through the motions when it comes to God?
- How do you ensure that your heart remains committed to Him?

Next Steps

Isaiah 29:13 reads, "The Lord says 'These people come near to me with their mouth and honor me with their lips, but their hearts are far from me. Their worship of me is made up only of rules taught by men.'" Today, be honest with yourself and examine whether your heart is with God or if you have found yourself engaging in religious ritual. If you have found the latter to be true, take the time to ask God for forgiveness; set aside the "religious" lifestyle, and seek a relationship with God that is as real as a relationship with a friend. You can do this by beginning to take His Word to heart and living what you say you believe. You can also do this by being honest with God about your thoughts, feelings, frustrations, etc., just as you would with a friend.

GOD MUST BE
THE LOVE OF YOUR LIFE

Hearing by the Word of God...

"Yet I hold this against you:
You have forsaken your first love" (Revelation 2:4).

When my husband and I met, we connected rather quickly. We met on a Christian dating website. He sent me a message that went something like this: "Has anyone swept you off your feet? If not, I have my broom". Yes, it was a corny line but he nabbed me with it. He lived in New York City while I was in Detroit. We spent many long nights talking. We emailed one another and sent text messages. This was before the day of the Smart Phone. When we were not speaking, emailing, or texting, I was thinking about him. I was listening to love songs; he definitely received a large amount of my attention. Is it not amazing the great impact love has on us?

Things were the same way when I made a commitment to Christ. I wanted to know all about God. I spent nights reading the Bible. I thought about how much He loved me and the many ways He had shown me. I dreamt about speaking to Him. My heart was consumed. I had never known a love like this. He had my heart—hook, line, and sinker. Our relationship was so important that I refused to allow anything to hinder it. But to my surprise, things did not remain this way.

Over time, I became busy and distracted. I did not spend as much time reading, praying, or seeking Him. The most important relationship of my life was pushed to the background. My Love sat at a distance, waiting for my return.

This poem demonstrates how distant my relationship with God became. I hope it will relay to you the importance of maintaining this connection. We cannot make our journeys to victory without Christ; it only comes through Him. No matter what our other commitments and responsibilities are, we need Him to be with us in our travels. We need Him to remain our First Love.

While reading this poem, put yourself in the midst of it as you reflect on its words.

My First Love

I remember when I first fell for You
At our beginning I was so unsure
Reluctant and even questioning
The time we spent together was at first small
I didn't know if I wanted to take the time or if I could
Give You all of me
But the more time we spent,
The more I had to be with You
I woke up thinking of You
And went to bed thinking of You
I even dreamed of talking to You
You began to show me the most intimate things about You
In your actions You showed me You cared
In Your Words You told me You loved me

You were my priority;
Nothing could stop me from getting to You
Then...
Life issues, busyness, and people came in the way
The very things You warned me about
But somehow I had forgotten

Where has it gone?
Why do You seem distant?
Why is it hard to get to You?
Now...
I miss the time we spent
I miss the late night talks

I miss Your touch
You said "away from me…I never knew you"
What happened? What went wrong?

I had forsaken my first Love, my Lord, my God and didn't
Even know…

"Yet I hold this against you: You have forsaken your first love"
(Revelation 2:4).

Self-Reflection Activity

Complete the following activity and be sure to journal your thoughts.

- Read the following scriptures and consider what they mean to you: Revelation 2:3-4.
- Have you allowed life's activities to impede your relationship with the Savior?
- Do you still value and consider your relationship with God as most important above all else?
- How can you take the time to remain connected to your First Love?

Next Steps

Revelation 2:4 reads, "Yet I hold this against you: You have forsaken your first love." Evaluate the current state of your relationship with Christ. Make needed changes in your priorities to put God as the focal point of your life. One way to do this is to ensure that you start your day by spending time in prayer and devotion.

CHRIST MUST LIVE, NOT YOU

Hearing by the Word of God...

"I have been crucified with Christ and I no longer live, but Christ lives in me. The life I live in the body, I live by faith in the Son of God, who loved me and gave himself for me" (Galatians 2:20).

When I bought my first house, I wanted it to remain as beautiful as when it was purchased. I wanted it to be well-maintained. Occasionally, my next door neighbor would enter the driveway and trample the lights that outlined my lawn. I became frustrated and made mention of it. I confronted her as respectful as possible, but it did not go well. She basically put me in my place and sent me away. Actually, her response was really colorful and very entertaining for the neighbors. One of my friends advised me to "give a gift in secret." I was a new believer and excited about what God was doing; but I was not willing to do that. I did not know how she would respond again, and frankly, I did not enjoy being embarrassed in front of the entire neighborhood. My friend explained that it was the right thing to do, as the Bible says, "A gift in secret pacifieth anger"

(Proverbs 21:14 KJV). Somewhat apprehensive, I bought a cake, put aside my feelings, and knocked on her door. I apologized and offered her the cake. She declined the cake, but was receptive. She shared with me some health problems and the fact that she was scheduled for surgery. She also shared some other hardships. I had no idea. I was adding stress to her situation because I was concerned for myself. I now understood her reaction.

That gift opened a door for God to work; rather, applying God's Word is what opened the door. After that day, we were on friendly terms; we talked about God and I prayed for her. We remained friendly for the rest of our time as neighbors. We also began making visits and looking out for each other. My selfishness almost caused me to miss the opportunity to crucify my flesh and to let the light of Christ shine in that situation. However, instead of continuing in pursuit of selfishness, I saw how a tensed situation was turned around and a caring relationship was established. It makes me wonder how many other opportunities I missed when I do not "die to self."

Have I Been Crucified?

> "I have been crucified with Christ and I no longer live, but Christ lives in me. The life I live in the body, I live by faith in the Son of God, who loved me and gave himself for me" (Galatians 2:20).

On one occasion, while reading the above scripture, I had to stop and ask myself, "Do these words mirror how I live as a Christian today?" When I examined my life, I found this statement was not entirely true for me. Upon dissecting this scripture, there are several statements that could be compared to my life. The first statement is, "I have been crucified with Christ and I no longer live..." The Bible says when Jesus was crucified, He gave up His Spirit. Can I say that I gave up my spirit? This is, of course, is in reference to the old nature that lived in me before I came to Christ. Did I give up my worldly desires in order to live a life pleasing to Christ, or am I still holding onto my old ways? Do I still want to do things in my own way, in my own timing? The answer to this question deals with self-will and obedience to God. If I let my desires overpower the will of God, I have not given up my old self. With my old self still "alive and kicking," Christ is not the one who dwells in me.

Who's Alive and Kicking?

Then Paul says, "... but Christ lives in me." When Jesus died, He became alive by the Spirit and was resurrected. If I died, then I should be made alive by His Spirit and resurrected as a new creation. The old nature is gone, and the new has arrived. If this is the case, then His Spirit is freely flowing within me. So I had to ask, "Does His new Spirit actively live in me? Do I keep Him dormant and unable to accomplish God's will in my life? If my victory comes through Christ, then whose will should I be accomplishing? His will or mine's?"

I learned that I must allow His Spirit to produce in me His fruit of " love, joy, peace, patience, kindness, goodness, faithfulness, gentleness, and self–control" (Galatians 5:22–23).

Am I producing the opposite? Instead of the fruit of the Spirit, am I producing the worldly fruit like "idolatry and witchcraft; hatred, discord, jealousy, fits of rage, selfish ambition, dissensions, factions and envy; drunkenness, orgies, and the like"

(Galatians 5:20-21)? Am I exposing others to a character that does not reflect Christ at all? Granted, I know that most Christians are not involved in drunkenness and orgies; but do I find myself placing anything higher than God? For example, do I place my job, house, husband, or children higher, knowing that anything that is put before or in the place of God is idolatry? Do I find myself manipulating situations or people? What about selfish ambition or jealousy, or causing discord among fellow believers? What about envying others? Am I finding myself producing such bitter fruit? I have to examine myself and really think about these things. Am I allowing Christ to live in me and produce His fruit? You must ask yourself the same questions.

A Life by Faith in Christ

The last statement that Paul makes in his declaration can only be lived out if the first two are true: "The life I live in the body, I live by faith in the Son of God, who loved me and gave himself for me" (Galatians 2:20). If it is I who lives and not the Spirit in me, then I cannot live by faith. Faith is something that comes from the heart. The Spirit testifies to our spirit the things of God, and thus faith is produced. So the last question becomes, "Am I truly walking this walk by faith?" Why is any of this important? Because it is what Jesus instructed us to do. Take a look at the following scripture.

> "...If anyone would come after me, he must deny himself and take up his cross and follow me. For whoever wants to save his life will lose it, but whoever loses his life for me and for the gospel will save it. What good is it for a man to gain the whole world, yet forfeit his soul?" (Mark 8:34b-36).

Jesus told us that we must daily sacrifice our will and desires in order to follow Him. Living according to God's will is how we obtain our victories. Since our victories rest within Christ, we ought to be willing to follow Him.

Willing to Follow Christ

When we look at scripture, we will see that after Jesus received the Holy Spirit, the Spirit immediately led Him, even into the wilderness. I am not sure about you, but a wilderness would not be my choice destination. I am pretty sure Jesus knew when He came upon that desert, it was not the most favorable place. In fact, we are on a similar journey ourselves. Have you ever noticed that sometimes you find yourself in a wilderness situation? Most times, we are running as fast as we can to get out. Jesus, however did not. He followed the Spirit there and endured the test and temptations. As scary as it may be, we must lay down our desires in order to follow after Christ. We must go where the Spirit leads. Not only did He tell us to take up our cross and follow Him, but He told us to do it daily. I believe the reason He told us to do it daily is because it is easily forgotten. Maybe we do not want to do so, but the fact remains that this practice is essential to our spiritual growth, even for our travels.

The statement, "take up the cross," implies action on our part; in order to take action, we have to be willing. There are benefits of being willing to follow God. In fact, Isaiah said when we are willing and obedient, we will eat the best of what the land bears (Isaiah 1:19).

Do not misunderstand me. I am not saying that this is a piece of cake. I know from personal experience. Even our Lord wrestled with His flesh; but He also gave us assurance that as He overcame, we too can overcome. The cross was not easy for Him to face. Before being crucified, Jesus did not want to bear the burden of death. He said, "not as I will, but as you will" (Matthew 26:39). Can you say the same? In my example, I learned that my journey will likely cross paths with those who need Christ. If I insist on doing my will and refusing His will, people will not experience Him through me. Jesus' motive was to please the Father. Is our love for God strong enough for us to say, "Not my will but yours?" Are we willing to take up our crosses and do what Jesus did? Can we allow His Spirit to live in us in order that His fruit can be produced in us? We do not want to ultimately lose our souls in an attempt to save our wills. Let Christ live in you.

Self-Reflection Activity

Complete the following activity and be sure to journal your thoughts.

- Read the following scriptures and consider what they mean to you: Galatians 2:20; Mark 8:34 – 36.
- Do you see yourself as really having been crucified with Christ? Have you given up your will in submission to Christ's?
- What can you do to daily remind yourself, "not my will but yours be done?"

Next Steps

Mark 8:34 reads, "Then he called the crowd to him along with his disciples and said: "If anyone would come after me, he must deny himself and take up his cross and follow me." Selfish ambition hinders us from being able to live as Jesus lived; so our goal today is to begin the practice of setting aside selfish ambition to follow Christ. This means serving Christ by serving others, and placing others above ourselves and practicing humility.

LIVE DIRECTED BY THE SPIRIT

Hearing by the Word of God...

"So I say, live by the Spirit, and you will not gratify the desires of the sinful nature" (Galatians 5:16).

I was blessed to have a surrogate grandmother, and by that I mean we were not blood-related. My mom was young and had the task of raising me alone; and yet this woman took us in and treated us like family, even though we were strangers. Even as a little baby, my "grandmother" raised me as her own grand-daughter. As I became older, I failed to contact her as often as I should have, which she made mention of often.

My grandmother passed away unexpectedly. She was still in her early seventies and full of life. She loved to dance and travel, and enjoyed the company of friends. She retired and lived life to the fullest. One day while working, my grandmother spontaneously came to mind. This happened repeatedly within the same day. I thought it was because I had not called her back from the previous month. In fact, for two weeks, I received impressions of her, but I kept saying, "I will call," and had not. One day, the impression to call her was very persistent until I stopped what I was doing and called my aunt who was her caregiver. My grandmother had been hospitalized. Given a grave prognosis, my grandmother chose to go home. She did not want to spend her days in a hospital, and we all knew that. They had not given her beyond the next day. Two days later, I was able to travel back to my hometown to see her the day before she left us. I was able to talk to her, sing to her, and tell her that I loved her. I sat with her through the night and was there with family when she took her final breath. I was only able to do this because of the Spirit's persistent prodding, and I am so thankful for that.

This prompting really started about two years prior to her death. The same type of persistent impression came to heart and mind. I knew God was leading me in this, but I was not sure why. I made it my business to call and talk to her periodically. I had moved to another state, so phone conversations were the best I could do. Shortly after these promptings began, I learned she had been in an accident. Things went from calling her while she was on the go to talking to her while she was bedridden. She progressively began to lose use of her feet, legs, and finally her hands. However, I was able to talk to her and she shared her faith with me.

Her trust in God was strong. She told me of how God was her Provider. She shared several stories I had not known. I was able to ask her why she helped so many people. She explained to me that it was her gift.

During the initial promptings, I had no idea what was coming in just two years. Because of the Holy Spirit's leading, I was able to talk to my grandmother more than I had in all of my adult life. I am convinced the last two years with my grandmother was a result of the Holy Spirit's leading. In fact, I am sure His promptings were to allow me to see her one last time. If ever there was a time I needed to be led by the Holy Spirit, it was then, and I am so grateful He did.

The Law or the Spirit?

Many of us have repeatedly heard that we are not governed by the Law because of grace in Christ Jesus. In fact, in Paul's letter to the Galatians, he strongly warned them against attempting to live according to the law. But since we are no longer under the law, how else are we governed if we are not living by a set of rules?

I had learned the answer to my questions: Christians are supposed to live according to the Holy Spirit. For years I struggled with this concept. I wanted to live a life committed to God and do what pleases Him. On one hand, from my experience in trying to live by different sets of rules, I would do well for a while. I would grow weary and feel exhausted in trying to obey the rules. I eventually considered the rules as a form of bondage. On the other hand, I would see others effortlessly "walk with God," and they seemed to be caught up in this free flow, full of peace and joy. How did they do it?

The Holy Spirit Leads Us into Truth

Scripture says there is a way that was opened to us by Christ, and that way by His Spirit. He made it so that when we become His disciples, the Holy Spirit comes to live inside of us. I knew this, yet, I still did not understand how I could "live" by the Spirit. I eventually realized that one of the Holy Spirit's purposes is to lead us into all truth. Now I understand why Jesus told Nicodemus no one can enter God's Kingdom unless he has been born of both the water and the Spirit (John 3:1-8). We can in no way please God within ourselves. Left alone, we cannot obey the entire law. Jesus sent the Holy Spirit to help us and guide us among other things. He said, "I will not leave you as orphans." He knew we needed help, so He sent the Spirit of Truth to guide us on our journeys. God delights when we live our lives following after the Holy Spirit because then we are living by truth. This is the key to understanding how we can please God without living by a set of rules.

Fulfilling the Spirit's Desires

Understanding that the Holy Spirit is here to lead us is not enough. We must also set our minds on what the Spirit desires. Think about when we lived in sin; at the time, we were slaves to sin. When we were slaves to sin, we did not have to make ourselves sin or live by the laws of sin. When we were slaves to sin, we willingly fulfilled the sinful desires of our flesh. But in Christ, sin no longer has mastery over us.

"Through Christ Jesus the law of the Spirit of life set me free from the law of sin and death"(Romans 8:2).

We are set free from sin. How wonderful! Now, we are new creations in Christ. Now that we are new creations in Christ, why do we try to make ourselves live by a written code, especially when the Holy Spirit is here to help us? Is it because we have not become slaves to righteousness? As the Bible instructs, those who focus on the flesh find themselves living according to the flesh and thus fulfilling its desires. However, those who focus on the Spirit find themselves living according to the Spirit, and thus fulfilling what the Spirit desires (Romans 8:5-6). Therefore, the determining factor is whether we are focused on our flesh or on the Holy Spirit.

Because there are so many distractions and detours on our journey, it is important to set our hearts and minds on the desires of the Holy Spirit. As we are focused in this way, we begin to notice His gentle promptings, leading us. Soon, we find ourselves effortlessly fulfilling the righteous requirements of the law. Soon, we find ourselves exactly where God wants us on this path. We are able to do this because the Spirit is leading us and no longer our flesh.

Spirit or Flesh?

Do you notice how there was no human effort of following the law of sin? We were innately submitted to it because that sinful nature lived in us. There should be no human effort in following God's righteous law if we allow the Holy Spirit to live in us. Allowing the Spirit to live within means following when

He leads. Just as the former nature fulfilled its sinful law, our new nature fulfills its righteous law. Just as the former state was normal to us, the new nature will become increasingly instinctive because we are submitted to God's Spirit. Who will we allow to win? Will it be the former nature or the new nature? We will find the key is to remove our focus from our flesh, because its desires deceive us. We must set our focus on God. Then we will hear the voice of the Spirit living in us. We will recognize His promptings. We will have "eyes to see and ears to hear" what the Spirit says. So here is the question: Will the submission to the Holy Spirit's leading ever become as effortless as when we lived in submission to our sinful nature? I believe so as we find ourselves yielding more and more to Him.

Self-Reflection Activity

Complete the following activity and be sure to journal your thoughts.

- Read the following scriptures and consider what they mean to you: Galatians 3:2–5; Galatians 3:10; Galatians 5:16–18; Romans 8:1–14.
- Do you find myself stressed out because you're trying to live by a set of rules?
- Do you trust that God's Spirit can lead you to accomplish His will?
- Are you ready to live your life dependent on the leading of God?

Next Steps

Proverbs 3:6 KJV reads, "In all thy ways acknowledge him, and he shall direct thy paths." Begin to seek God for His personal instruction for your life. Ask Him for direction, and take the time to listen for the response.

BE WASHED
BY THE WORD

Hearing by the Word of God...

*"Christ loved the church and gave himself up for her to make her
holy, cleansing her by the washing with water through the word"
(Ephesians 5:25–26).*

When children play outdoors, there is no guess work
needed to figure out where they have been. They usually come home dirty from head to toe. When my oldest son
reached an age when he could play outside during daycare, by
the end of the day, he looked like he had never been washed.
My son often times came home with woodchips from the play-
ground embedded in his clothing. Like a good mommy, I rou-
tinely bathed him and washed his clothes. Sometimes I did not
have the time or energy to fully bathe him, so I would only wash
the essential parts and put fresh clothing on him, although
this only covered the dirt temporarily.

Exposed to Outside Elements

Our spirit is also affected in the same way by the world in which we live. Now that living in sin is considered the "norm," it is normal to be exposed to it daily. Like children playing outdoors, sometimes we are tempted to play around in the dirt, or we resist the temptation but are still affected due to its proximity. Think of the times you have been outside with the wind blowing. When you come inside, suddenly you notice a scent you had not recognized previously. You may have noticed particles in your hair or dirt on your clothes. To get rid of the dirt and the scent, you wash it away. In the same way, there is great importance in washing our spirit daily with the water of God's Word.

Washed by the Word

The Bible says, "Christ loved the church and gave himself up for her to make her holy, cleansing her by the washing with water through the word" (Ephesians 5:25–26). Jesus knew that without allowing God's Word to cleanse us, the residue of the world would remain on us. This residue hinders us from becoming the church that God desires, one that is pure, holy, and set apart unto God. Before Jesus faced His ultimate sacrifice, He showed us the importance of this process. He attempted to wash the feet of His disciples; and when Peter declined, He told him, "Unless I wash you, you have no part with me" (John 13:8).

Do Not Skip the Process

If we are not careful to take heed to what Jesus said, the stench of the world will affect us. If we let the world's residue build, the results are not pretty. Eventually, the stench will be very evident to ourselves and those around us. The influence of the world slowly creeps up on us. And before you know it, we find ourselves living and responding in ways that we thought were left behind. If we are not careful, we will notice the change and wonder what happened. We may say, "Why was I so mean to the cashier?" or "Why am I starting to worry more?" I have said it before and will say it again. Our victory comes through following Christ. When He gave Himself to make us holy, He did not leave it there; He also purified us by the Word of God.

In the Old Testament, the emphasis was not only on offering sacrifices for sins, but also being purified from becoming unclean. Anytime a person was exposed to something unclean, they became unclean. They needed to offer a sacrifice and submit themselves to a time of cleansing and purification. This is what Jesus demonstrated when He gave Himself and began cleansing the Church with the Word. This is why the Word of God is essential to our journey. If not careful to apply this process of cleansing, we will find ourselves going down the wrong path.

Learn from What I Failed to Do

I have experienced what it is like to be impacted by the world around me. There was an extended period of time when my job was almost unbearably challenging. Things were so hectic and the stress level was so extremely high that I felt like I was in a pressure cooker. The busier I got, the less time I spent in quality time with God's Word. My spirit had become filthy, and it was very evident in how I dealt with the pressures. While I never swore or belittled anyone, I surely let them have it. I sent emails that I know the Holy Spirit advised me not to send. I became a regular contributor to voicing my opinions and complaints with co-workers. My demeanor changed and my countenance showed my frustration. I wore my aggravation on my sleeve and I wore it well. However, I would go home and become frustrated with myself because I knew that I was not being a good representation of God.

What happened? I had not spent sufficient time in God's Word to allow it to wash me. Simply attending church and listening to a sermon was not enough. Even halfheartedly glancing at scriptures without meditation or contemplation on the meaning did not do the job. It became obvious that emerging myself in God's purifying Word was essential to me in my successful travels down this road to victory. Likewise, it is essential for yours as well. My challenge to you is to make the commitment to bathe in the Word of God often. In doing this, you are allowing it to perform its purifying work.

Self-Reflection Activity

Complete the following activity and be sure to journal your thoughts.

- Read the following scriptures and consider what they mean to you: Ephesians 5:25-27; John 13:3-10; John 15:3.
- Do you honestly spend time studying, meditating, and learning how to apply God's Word?
- Do you take God's Word to heart?

Next Steps

John 13:8 reads, "...Jesus answered, 'Unless I wash you, you have no part with me.'" We can get so caught up in our responsibilities that we neglect the Word of God. Find creative ways to study and apply God's Word on a consistent basis. For example, since I have two young children, it is hard to get in any personal time. My resolve was to buy an electronic reader so that I can carry my books around with me. As a result, when I am waiting around for something, I can just pull out the reader and allow myself to be washed by His Word.

REMAIN PREPARED FOR JESUS' RETURN

Hearing by the Word of God...

"Watch therefore, for you do not know what hour your Lord is coming. But know this, that if the master of the house had known what hour the thief would come, he would have watched and not allowed his house to be broken into.

Therefore you also be ready, for the Son of Man is coming at an hour you do not expect" (Matthew 24:42-44 NKJV).

I am normally a planner. It does not matter if I am on the job or off, I try to have all of my ducks in a row. I am detailed no matter what I am doing. Planning kid's birthday parties, holiday gatherings, and vacations all require detail. This is usually done well in advance. I like to be prepared. One year our family was so busy that I could not plan for everything. Something had to be neglected. That year, it was our paid family vacation. As it would happen, I worked until the very hour that we needed leave. I had not packed. I normally pack for myself and our sons. Yet, I had not packed for any of us. I usually print a check-list of items specific to the type of vacation. I had not done that either. We were going on a week-long cruise and the bags were empty. I am not sure what I was thinking. I guess I figured as long as we had passports and credit cards, if we missed something, it was not a big deal. My dear seven-year-old son volunteered to pack items for himself and his brother.

I finally finished working, logged off the computer, and proceeded to finally pack. I even double-checked my kid's items. Everything was thrown in the bags, but we had what we needed. We got on the road, and the next day boarded the ship. We enjoyed ourselves and the other members of our group. We arrived to our first port of call, Key West Florida. I discovered that I had forgotten the beach shoes but not a big deal, we could go without them. We arrived at the beach, only to find it full of rocks. (Who knew the beaches in Key West were rocky? Well, I did not know.) That beach visit was not so much fun.

Our vacation continued, and around day four, my son ran out of underwear. This was not good but we improvised until I could use the ship's laundry facility. Then we arrived in Nassau, Bahamas. I had not planned our excursion. My thoughts were to find an islander and ask about a nice beach. We were told one was within walking distance, and after walking about two miles we arrived at a beach filled with garbage, broken glass, and adult partying. This was not a good place for the kids. But our vacation was not ruined. We visited one beach that we enjoyed and had fun on the ship. I use this only as an illustration of how being unprepared can be a hindrance. When it comes to our journey with Christ, being unprepared could lead to a more detrimental disappointment.

Jesus is Coming Back

One very early morning after feeding my newborn son and drifting back off to sleep, I heard a voice say, "And tell them I'm coming back!" In my sleepiness, I did not realize what I had heard at first; then I woke up in pure excitement because I realized that I had actually heard the Lord speak. As I pondered this, I wondered what it meant, and more importantly, what was I supposed to do with it. Then a couple of days later, I found out that our Sunday school program began a series on the very same subject. I was really excited, but then I realized that the return of my Lord was not at the forefront of my Christianity. I had no longer been mindful of Jesus' return, something that I was previously watchful for.

A Forgotten Reality

What is the ultimate purpose of salvation if not the culmination of being with our Savior? I know that salvation is much more than being Heaven bound; but even in that thinking, somewhere in our Christian journey, we tend to lose sight of the fact that one day our Lord will return. In all of the ups and downs we experience, the busy nature of our lives, whether working, taking care of family, or serving, the primary reason for our salvation is forgotten.

A Time of Preparation

Our journey to victory requires preparation on our part. Yes, we do have some responsibilities and that is to prepare for His return. Jesus said He was going to prepare a place for us. He is making special provisions for His bride. As one who is part of His bride, am I also preparing for Him as well? In Matthew chapters twenty-four and twenty-five, Jesus uses a series of parables to help us understand the importance of being prepared for His return. In the parable about the owner of the house, Jesus told us that if the house's owner had known when the thief was coming, he would have waited for him so that he could not break in. Think about it: The owner only protects the house when he knows there will be a robbery; otherwise, he is not protecting the house.

In the parable of the faithful servant, Jesus speaks of two contrasting hearts and motives toward the master. The committed servant was described as wise and faithful. The other servant did deeds of darkness, and Jesus called him foolish.

In yet another parable about ten virgins, the bridegroom took long in his coming. Some of the ladies were prepared with extra oil for their lamps while others did not bring extra. The ones who were prepared, Jesus called wise; and the ones who were not prepared, He called foolish. Because these virgins were not prepared, they missed the coming of the bridegroom and were not able to go with him.

Anticipate, Commit, and Remain Faithful

In telling these parables, Jesus gave us a very strong message. These three parables tell me that I should be anticipating Jesus' return. In my anticipation, I should remain prepared and committed for the long haul. Finally, it is my job to put to use the "talents" He's given me. Looking at each of the characters in these parables, it leads me to ask myself, "Am I only faithful when I know He is soon to return?" or "Am I ready to be faithful in the long haul?" I believe the reason why Jesus told us of His return in several ways is so His return will always be of great importance to us. He did not want us to forget and become comfortable in this world, but to look to eternity ahead. Looking forward to eternity with Him should always be set within our hearts. Will you faithfully continue your journey and prepare for His return?

Self-Reflection Activity

Complete the following activity and be sure to journal your thoughts.

- Read the following scriptures and consider what they mean to you: John 14:2-3; Matthew 24:36-51; Matthew 25:1-13.
- Is the return of Jesus still of most importance to you?
- When He returns, will He find you doing what He has told you to do?
- How can you use the gifts and talents He gave you to tell others about His gift of salvation?
-

Next Steps

Matthew 28:19 reads, "Therefore go and make disciples of all nations." Remember that it is our job to introduce the world to Christ. He will return one day, and those who do not accept Him will be condemned. Allow God to touch your heart for the sake of others so that you freely share your faith. Today, share the gospel of Jesus Christ with someone.

LESSON TWENTY ONE

KEEP YOUR EYES
ON THE PRIZE

Hearing by the Word of God...

*"Then I saw a new heaven and a new earth, for the first heaven and
the first earth had passed away, and there was no longer any sea. I
saw the Holy City, the New Jerusalem, coming down out of heaven
from God, prepared as a bride beautifully dressed for her husband.
And I heard a loud voice from the throne saying,*

*'Now the dwelling of God is with men, and he will live with them.
They will be his people, and God himself will be with them and be
their God. He will wipe every tear from their eyes. There will be no
more death or mourning or crying or pain, for the old order of
things has passed away'" (Revelation 21:1–4).*

This is one of my favorite scripture passages in the Bible.
We get such a beautiful description of the prize for those
who "overcome." We get to live in the New Jerusalem. On that
day, the earth as we know it will be gone and there will be a
new earth. Everything will be made new. There will be no more
mourning, no more death, no more pain, and no more sorrow.
God will live in our midst, and we will belong to Him.

I think of this in light of all the pain that I have endured. I think of all of the suffering of mankind. I realize the true depth of God's love. It baffles me, despite how mankind has treated God, that He would give us such a wonderful offer. I know all the sins that I have committed, all of the disobedient acts I have committed, even as a Christian. I know that I do not deserve such treatment. I do not deserve to live in eternity with a Holy God. Yet, God offers it anyway.

We Have a Goal in Sight

Having the goal of eternal life with Him in sight ignites us and keeps us going. We need this picture and hope because somewhere in this Christian walk, we have pretty much realized that it is not going to be easy. We have to fight and sometimes suffer things undeservingly. We are stretched and challenged in our faith by trials and persecution. It seems as though no matter what we do, we cannot hide from these trials that seem so eager to test us. The Apostle Paul speaks of the things he encountered as he did for the sake of the Gospel.

A Shared Destiny

He said he did all of it to "share in the blessings" (1 Corinthians 9). Paul believed that sharing in the struggles of being connected with Christ is actually sharing in the blessing of Christ. Paul considered these struggles to be a part of his identification with Christ. He compared perseverance through the struggles with that of running a race. Paul had a reason for everything he did in Christ. This meant every jail he found himself thrown in, every beating, and every persecution, was all for the sake of the Gospel of Christ.

As with him, so it is with us. We may not be jailed or beaten, but we do endure persecution strictly because we belong to God. Sometimes it seems like all we do is "fight the good fight" because our "enemy the devil" is always prowling "around like a lion looking for someone to devour." As we continue to look to Christ and remember how He endured, we can remember our goal. One day, when all is said and done, God will wipe every tear from our eyes, and the struggle will be over. I want to share one more personal example from my life. This example comes from a dream.

Focused on the Finish Line

I once had a very colorful and vibrant dream. At the beginning, my mother and I were on our way to our destination. We were in this house that reminds me of stucco houses seen in other countries with windows but no glass. The house was a single story house and small in stature. We walked through the house and climbed out of the window. I remember us helping one another to climb out. As we continued, we were in what seemed like an open field, full of grass and flowers. It was a beautiful sight to behold. The picture was so beautiful that I often wish I had painting skills to replicate it. As we moved along, we met other women whom we eventually joined on their journey. The group grew to be a long line of women, moving hand and hand, making our journeys together. If we were facing north, then our group of ladies traveled eastward. To the north of us was a lake. All of us were intent on arriving to our destination. I got the impression the travel was not rushed but steady. Suddenly, from across the lake were arrows being launched against our travel band of ladies. This alarmed us, but we continued. Then one person received a word: "Do not pay attention to the arrows; they cannot hurt you." All were instructed to pass this message along. One by one, the message was passed in order to encourage each lady. The message was to keep us focused on the destination ahead, disallowing the attacks to distract us. It worked as we continued along our way.

The dream never really ended; the last memory I have were those words of encouragement. This dream is one of the reasons why I encourage other women in Christ. As I bring this book to an end, I can see clearly the dream's correlation to my life, even to this book. My job was to encourage you along the way that victory is ahead. So keep your eyes on the prize as you continue your journey to victory.

Self-Reflection Activity

Complete the following activity and be sure to journal your thoughts.

- Read the following scriptures and consider what they mean to you: 1 Corinthians 9:23-26a; Revelation 21: 1-5.
- Do you have your eyes on the promised eternity or on the things of this world?
- Are you willing to share in the struggles that come along with being a follower of Christ?

Next Steps

Philippians 3:12–14 reads, "Not that I have already obtained all this, or have already been made perfect, but I press on to take hold of that for which Christ Jesus took hold of me. Brothers, I do not consider myself yet to have taken hold of it. But one thing I do: Forgetting what is behind and straining toward what is ahead, I press on toward the goal to win the prize for which God has called me heavenward in Christ Jesus." Put the reality of our eternity in Christ always before you. Never forget that we are strangers in this world, but that our permanent home is with Christ.

ROAD MARKERS

We have come to the end of our journey together, but really it is just the beginning of your own personal trek down Victory's Road. I want to leave you with one more thought: "Whatever is true, whatever is noble, whatever is right, whatever is pure, whatever is lovely, whatever is admirable–if anything is excellent or praiseworthy–think about such things" (Philippians 4:8). Changing our thinking is a part of growing while we travel through life. Replacing negative thoughts with God's truth is highly beneficial. Below are some short affirmations that relate to each lesson of this book. I pray they may help you find strength as you travel on your journey.

1. I have found life in Jesus.
2. He has drawn me by His love.
3. He has set me free from bondage.
4. He has brought me into His rest.
5. He takes care of the lilies, He will take care of me.
6. He has become my hope.
7. He delivered and protected me once, He will do it again.
8. He is greater than the one who is in the world and He lives in me.
9. He makes me stronger in my trials.
10. He turns my storms into spiritual growth.
11. He has victory in store for me if I persevere.
12. He is enabling me to bear the fruit of His Kingdom.

13. He never gives up on me.
14. He desires my heart.
15. He desires my complete faithfulness and obedience.
16. He desires to be my first Love.
17. He died for me, so my earthly self must die to truly serve Him.
18. His Spirit is in me to lead me.
19. He cleanses me with His Word.
20. He is coming back for me.
21. He is my crown of victory.

AFTERWORD

"Finally, be strong in the Lord and in his mighty power. Put on the full armor of God so that you can take your stand against the devil's schemes. For our struggle is not against flesh and blood, but against the rulers, against the authorities, against the powers of this dark world and against the spiritual forces of evil in the heavenly realms. Therefore put on the full armor of God, so that when the day of evil comes, you may be able to stand your ground, and after you have done everything, to stand. Stand firm then, with the belt of truth buckled around your waist, with the breastplate of righteousness in place, and with your feet fitted with the readiness that comes from the gospel of peace. In addition to all this, take up the shield of faith, with which you can extinguish all the flaming arrows of the evil one. Take the helmet of salvation and the sword of the Spirit, which is the word of God. And pray in the Spirit on all occasions with all kinds of prayers and requests. With this in mind, be alert and always keep on praying for all the saints" (Ephesians 6:10–18).

I cannot honestly write a book on triumph despite trials without mentioning the enemy to the Christian. There is a spiritual battle taking place even now, and many times our trials are a result of this fact. Though our struggles sometimes may appear to come from man, the Bible says that our struggle is not against "flesh and blood." Our struggle is actually against evil powers in high places. This book has provided a lead way into the only offensive weapon the believer has, the Word of God.

To combat our unseen enemy, it is also vital that we understand the importance of the defensive armor as well. The Bible says the battle is spiritual, so we must fight with spiritual weapons. Therefore, as Christians, it is greatly important that we put on all of God's armor each day. Therefore, as you go forth on your road to victory, take time to be armored fully. God bless.

ABOUT THE AUTHOR

Nicole C Calhoun lives near Dallas, Texas, with her husband and two children. She is a bible teacher and has an enthusiasm for helping women to understand and experience God's hope and restoration in their lives. This desire prompted her to become the founder of Restored to Stand Ministries, which is a Christian ministry dedicated to women.

For more information on speaking engagements and workshops, please visit the website or email:

nicole@restoredtostand.com
www.nicolecalhoun.com

To find other books by this author visit:
https://www.amazon.com/author/nicoleccalhoun

9 780990 542339